TUMBLEWEED

A BIOGRAPHY

Catherine de Hueck Doherty on the grounds of
Madonna House, Combermere

Tumbleweed

A Biography

By Eddie Doherty

MADONNA HOUSE PUBLICATIONS
Combermere, Ontario · Canada · K0J 1L0

Cover: Ed C. Hunt from original publication

Canadian Cataloguing in Publication Data
  Doherty, Eddie, 1890-1975
    Tumbleweed

New Canadian ed.
First published: Milwaukee, Wis.: Bruce Publ., 1948
ISBN 0-921440-12-X

    1. Doherty, Catherine de Hueck, 1896-1985.
2. Catholics — Biography.   I. Title.

BX4705.D64D64   1989   282'.092'4   C89-090035-3

Published originally by Bruce Publishing Company 1948
New Edition: Madonna House Publications 1989

ISBN 0-921440-12-X

MADONNA HOUSE PUBLICATIONS
COMBERMERE, ONTARIO
CANADA
K0J 1L0

This is the book of Catherine. Of her, the Rev. Paul H. Furfey once said, "She is God's own Tumbleweed, blowing through the world, wherever the breath of the Holy Ghost may send her."

To her, the book is affectionately dedicated.

Catherine 1942

Eddie Doherty Early 40's

1

"SEX," said the baroness in a loud and plangent voice, "is the chalice of the sacrament of matrimony."

Mr. Dee, slouched over a magazine in the back room of the library, straightened up and listened.

"Without sex there is no sacrament, there is no marriage. Sex is beautiful. God made it for us to enjoy. It is holy. Of course, like all holy things, it can be, and is, profaned. You profane it when you say it is dirty, or when you think it evil."

Mr. Dee could not see the woman to whom the baroness was talking. He wasn't interested in her; and he had a knack of not seeing anything except that which interested him. But he felt something like pity for her. She had deliberately placed herself in the path of a verbal avalanche, but without realizing her danger. Now let her try to catch her breath if she could, before she was buried in the blonde Russian's word-fall!

It was the baroness who absorbed Mr. Dee's attention. Another woman saying such things, he felt, would have lowered her voice, might have spoken in a whisper to make sure she was not overheard by anyone except the visitor. Apparently the Russian didn't care who heard her. If her audience were embarrassed, that was too bad; but sometimes one remembers a lesson only because of the smart it engendered.

And, if others listened, they could learn something too. Maybe they needed the lecture as well as the woman who had evoked it.

Then too, it was usually necessary for the baroness to raise her voice. Streetcars were forever rattling by in 135th Street. Boys and girls were screaming at some game that kept them running through the traffic. Taxis and trucks and pleasure cars kept honking in alarm and anger. A child with the instincts of a hotcha drummer spent hours beating the side of a garbage can set precariously on the edge of the curb. Women called shrilly from windows across the way. Drunks sang in hideous disharmony outside the blue door. And there was always the barking of some dog, or the cry of some peddler sitting on a horse-drawn cart or wagon, to compete with the speaker for attention.

Mr. Dee could hear perfectly.

"Why do you think there are so many divorces in this country? One out of three! Divorces. Abortions. Prostitution everywhere. It's because people think that sex is dirty. Jokes against marriage in the newspapers, in the magazines, in best-selling books, and hour after filthy hour on the radio until your heart smokes with fury! I can understand that about pagans. But we are supposed to be a Christian people. We are supposed to know that sex is clean, joyous, natural, a glorious gift of God."

Mr. Dee had never seen the baroness angry before. She seemed to live in a restrained joyousness — in a happiness so intense it frequently bubbled out of her wide mouth in peals of laughter, or shone out of her eyes in a burst of bright blue glory.

An extremely passionate woman, he decided. An emotional woman, but sane and logical even in anger. He studied the lines in her face. She had suffered much, evidently. Her wisdom sprang out of her life, not out of the books she had read nor the teachers to whom she had listened. She spoke with an authority that only a harrowing existence could have conferred.

"To say it is a duty you owe your husband, or a task imposed on women for the creation of children — and nothing else — is blasphemy. Sheer blasphemy. I'm so sick of hearing about cold women, prudish women, women who think God blushes every time they strip themselves for the bath. The fools! These are the women who have brought more misery to the world than all your prostitutes. Don't try to tell me about them. I've talked to hundreds of them in the hospital. I talk to them every day, here in Friendship House.

"A woman who thinks that sex is dirty makes her life a stinking hell. She profanes a sacrament. She drives her husband into adultery, or worse. She brings up dirty-minded, cold, fearful little boys and girls. She makes God's idea of marriage a trick of the devil. I have no patience with her. I cannot forgive her ignorance. She should know better.

"In Poland, on the wedding night, bride and bridegroom get down on their knees, after their first union, and sing a *Te Deum,* a psalm of thanks to almighty God for the beautiful gift with which He has blessed them. Now go back to your husband, and tell him you've been a fool. Start another honeymoon and make it last. It is your right, your sacred privilege. It should be a great and holy joy."

Mr. Dee didn't see the prudish wife leave. He was wrapped in his own moody thoughts, and in a sort of wonder at this Russian baroness. What had brought her here to Harlem? What had induced her to live with the Negroes, in a Negro neighborhood, in the poverty of the Negroes, and in the love of the Negroes? What had inspired her to give her life to them?

There was a story in this woman, Catherine. And he had only an inkling of it. She had been a noblewoman in Russia.

She had been a Red Cross nurse in the Russian army during World War I. She had been rich. Very rich. She had fled her native land during the Bolshevik revolution. She had lived in Canada. She had lectured all over Canada and the United States. She had worked at menial tasks. She had made a lot of money in New York — and had given up everything she had, to live in poverty and help the poor.

The Baroness Catherine de Hueck was beautiful with an old-world beauty. High cheek bones. A wide high forehead. The biggest head and the stubbornest chin Mr. Dee had ever seen on a woman. Her hair was braided and arranged in a coronet. It was three shades of shining gold. She wore blue earrings, which made her eyes seem even bluer than they were. She used lipstick and rouge. Her fingers were ink-stained, and there was a dab of ink on the bare elbow that stuck out of the hole in her blue sweater. She wore a rough brown-checked skirt that looked as old as the sweater, torn cotton stockings, and disconsolate-looking shoes. Her clothes might have come out of a rag bag; but she wore them with distinction.

She was big, but she was graceful. She was plump, but full of energy. She was dominant, and humble. She was poised and calm now — after her impromptu lecture — yet ready to attack again if need be. She never pulled a punch.

She had surrounded herself with half a dozen or more young men and women — kids who seemed as eager as herself, Mr. Dee thought, to serve the poor. She ruled them with affection, and with rigor. She cooked for them. She dressed them in secondhand clothes. She worked them hard. She expected them to be as poor, as reliant on God for everything, as busy, as intelligent, and as happy as herself. She scolded them and petted them. She bossed them and she mothered them. She was impatient with their faults — and intolerant of their puns

— yet quick to console and to advise them in their hours of worry or sorrow.

She spoke nine languages. Her vocabulary of English words was a rich and colored arabesque, inlaid with the slang of many trades and professions, studded with the racy argot of Harlem, and ornamented here and there with a Damn, or a Hell, or a Baloney, or a Bosh!

Surely hers was no ordinary story, Mr. Dee reflected. He was wasting time, sitting here in the back room of the library, however. If he wanted the story he must get it over a table in a restaurant, or during a ride in the car — say up the Hudson Parkway or the Boston Post Road — or some other spot far away from this busy Friendship House.

Mr. Dee was something of a newspaperman, and stories were the breath of life to him. He had been gathering them for a quarter of a century or more; and hoped to spend his life in that pursuit. He was fifty or so at this time. His hair was a mixture of silver and black and gray; and his triangular bristle of mustache was a blend of rust and rime. He was something like six feet in height, but he walked with a slouch which made him seem less tall. He was pigeon-toed, and strolled through life with his head down. His eyes looked sleepy most of the time, but they saw what they wanted to see.

He wore a heavy military coat. Apparently he had been a war correspondent. And he carried a bright red muffler over his left shoulder. People frequently stopped him on the street, elderly women usually — but sometimes a pretty girl — and said, "You're going to lose it, Mister." But he wasn't going to lose it. It had been passed through a loop in the shoulder of the coat. It was firmly fastened. He liked it that way. It was convenient, he said, and it gave him something of a dash. He dressed in gray tweeds, and he usually smoked a briar pipe —

though he sometimes smoked as many cigarettes as the baroness herself.

The baroness liked him, he knew, and that pleased him. He was aware that he puzzled her too. That pleased him more. It was good, he had learned, to be a mystery to a woman. The less he revealed about himself the more she wanted to know. He intended to keep it that way.

Eventually, when he had learned to call her by her first name, he invited her to a late dinner in a little café in Manhattan.

"You look tired, Catherine. And even haggard. You need a good thick steak — and maybe something to drink?"

"Gosh, yes," she exploded, springing out of her chair, "that's exactly what I need."

There were other cafés and other nights. They sat and talked, here and there and elsewhere. Mr. Dee ate and drank and listened, Catherine nibbled and sipped and talked.

Sometimes peculiar idioms and queer twists of speech crept into her talk. She mispronounced words — purposely, Mr. Dee thought, in an effort to make him laugh. "And then I stepped in a mud poodle." "Well, I am only a spook in a wheel." Sometimes she spoke in a stately prose that was akin to heroic blank verse. Sometimes she used gestures to emphasize her words. Sometimes there were tears in her eyes, sometimes immeasurable joy.

Mr. Dee worked smoothly, here and there and elsewhere, in New York or Chicago, or wherever they might be together, to sate his curiosity. And he worked patiently, without haste. There was no deadline for this story; but he must have it whole. With all the detail he could gather.

It came in snatches and at long intervals. And sometimes it was interrupted by the clang of a fire engine hurrying through a busy street, by the raucous call of a lonely tugboat in the river, or by little knots of men who had listened avidly to the plangent voice and gathered around the table to ask questions.

The story was years in the telling, and it began with the words:

"When I first went to war . . ."

2

THE world was white and clean when she first went to war; and life spoke to her gaily, promising exciting things. She was fifteen or sixteen. She was tall and willowy and incredibly strong. Her eyes were a royal blue. Her hair gleamed with three shades of gold. And her laugh was musical.

She was the daughter of one of the Czar's ablest diplomats, a retired colonel of hussars, Theodore de Kolyschkine; and the bride of Baron Boris de Hueck, one of the richest men in Russia. She was a Red Cross nurse.

She was assigned to a quiet sector. The work was interesting, delightful, and absurdly easy. She was attached to the medical section, and also to the commissary, of a unit of the First Army, and her main task was connected with the feeding of the men. Nursing, at this time, was a secondary task, and a light one. It was early in 1916, and there were few casualties in the camp.

She was to see that each man received two and a half pounds of bread per meal, three lumps and a fraction of sugar, a bowl of soup, and all the tea he could drink; therefore she must be sure there was always enough food on hand, not only for her own unit, but for such other troops as might arrive.

She was in charge of the cooks and bakers, the over-age soldiers, men of fifty and older, and those who handed out the rations to the men and served the officers.

The men usually ate in the open, squatting around bonfires that had been kindled in the snow. There was a shack for the officers, and long tables covered with oilcloth. The food was a little better in the shack, but only a little better.

She found it interesting to watch the officers playing chess or checkers or other indoor games, to take a hand in their games, or to listen to their chatter. But it was fun to talk to the men, to listen to their music, and to watch their horseplay.

There was plenty of time for recreation, for studies — she was taking several courses in the Imperial Russian University — for letter writing, for long walks, for prayers, and for dances.

Sometimes a dance for the officers and nurses would last until late hours. An orchestra organized among the cooks and bakers and orderlies might furnish the music; or there might be some military band available.

There was always music. There was always song. There was always a mild excitement in the camp, and the feeling of stirring adventures to come.

Sometimes the young nurse would be awakened by the ringing of a phone, to be told that a regiment would be at the depot within a few hours and everything must be prepared. She would rush out, wake the cooks and bakers, get the fires lighted in the rolling kitchens, and make sure everything was ready.

Presently, far off, she would hear the sound of men's voices, singing of a maiden with dark eyes, or the girl who loved a Cossack, or the beauties of the steppes. Then would come the tramp of marching feet, the shouts of officers, the creak of wagons, the jingle of chains, and the smell of horseflesh. Almost before she realized it, musical instruments would be twanging all over the camp, a thousand men would be singing — different songs in different keys — and shadowy figures would begin lining up and coming forward into the light of the oil lamps and candles.

Laughing, clean-shaven boys, going to the front; or bearded and weary and bloodstained men coming back for their relief, or hurrying in retreat from battle.

They were all beautiful under the glittering stars, she thought, old or young, alert or weary. Her heart would swell, contemplating as they wolfed their food, or slept, rolled up in their wool or sheepskin cloaks; for they were as much a part of her beloved Russia as the plains, the rivers, the mountains. And it was a privilege to serve them.

Men came and ate and sang and slept and disappeared, giving place to others. It was more like a daily military pageant than a war. So it was difficult to realize that war was just over the horizon.

Catherine sensed danger only from the amorous and lonely officers attached to the unit, and from some of the young lieutenants passing through.

There was a medical officer who wrote her impassioned sonnets and who looked at her intently, if slyly, when he was alone with her — yet never uttered any of the love words he had written. There were two who had threatened to fight a duel for her affections. There were scores who begged her, now and then, for a kind word or a kiss. And there was one who kissed her thoroughly — though she never found out who he was.

A contingent of nurses had stopped overnight at the camp, on the way to the battle lines, and took up all the available beds. The personnel of the unit were billeted, temporarily, in a vacant hayloft.

"Men on the right," an officer said. "Women on the left."

"On the left of what?" Nurse de Hueck asked him; but he

had vanished into the night and the howling wind without bothering to answer.

She went into the barn. She saw a ladder and climbed it to the loft. She found a canvas screen just above the top rung, and thrust her hand through its opening.

"Help me up," she whispered.

"Who is it?" someone asked.

"Nurse de Hueck."

Before she realized it was a man's voice she heard, before she could retreat, or say "Sorry, I'm on the wrong ladder," a pair of arms was fastened about her, and a mustached face was kissing her again and again.

She was helpless. She couldn't move her pinioned arms. She couldn't move her head, as she had tried to do, in an effort to bite. She couldn't retreat. And she couldn't cry out in protest because the man's mouth was tightly pressed against her own.

Eventually the man's arms loosened, and she slipped through them. She found the right ladder, and spent perhaps half an hour wondering how she could ever identify the man who had kissed her. All she knew about him was that he had a mustache.

The white world vanished a few months after Catherine first went to war. The air grew soft, luring, sentimental. And a morning arrived when there was nothing to do but saddle a horse and ride into the fresh young countryside.

The road was long and winding and beautiful. Trees were budding. Birds were singing, or streaking in gaudy flashes through the air. In the distance a clump of lilacs beckoned her.

She passed a deserted farmhouse. There was a wide ditch on three sides of it, and there were soldiers in the ditch. But she thought nothing of that. She was absorbed in the wonder of the lilacs.

A soldier stood up in the ditch and shouted to her, waving his arms. She waved to him, and sped on, wondering what he had said. The horse was galloping, enjoying the sunshine and the wind and the smell of the earth, even as his mistress enjoyed them.

Insects flew all around, above her head. She bent low. The insects flew lower. She tried to shoo them away with her hands. She could not see them, she could only hear the whine they made as they went by.

The lilacs were only a few yards ahead when she saw another soldier waving. And this time she heard what he said.

"The Germans," he shouted. "They're shooting at you, you little fool. Get off your horse and crawl on your belly."

The term he used for Germans meant "damn foreigners." Russians had no use for foreigners, especially those who came from Germany. They had always hated the Germans and had no such pet words for them as Jerries or Heinies or Fritzes. A German was either a German or a damned foreigner.

Catherine got off her horse, rolled into a ditch in her nice new uniform, and crawled back along the roadside for a mile or two. The horse turned around calmly and ambled back, keeping pace with his mistress.

Now and then she looked up, to see the damn foreigners lying in the open field, shooting at her. She was more shocked than frightened. It had never entered her mind that any man could deliberately shoot at a woman, especially a nurse.

She returned to camp to find everybody stirring. The unit was going closer to the front.

Adventure had come at last.

The whole First Army was advancing, moving slowly along the roads; the cavalry in front, the wagons behind, cumbersome covered wagons drawn by horses.

There were no motors on the Russian side that war, no fast-moving vehicles of any kind. Moving up meant about twenty miles a day. The horses, pulling tons and tons of supplies, could go no farther than that without killing themselves.

The medical unit stopped for tea in a village, and the officer in charge suggested the nurses might stay behind long enough for a swim.

"We have to rest the horses," he explained, "and you might just as well take the opportunity to wash the dust of the roads off your bodies."

There was a lake near the road, and the water was deep and cold.

Twelve women found a clump of trees, stripped off their clothes, and plunged in.

Catherine floated on her back, looking up at the fleecy white islands in the blue above her. The bright sun dazzled her. She closed her eyes — then opened them suddenly at a noise overhead.

"A plane," she cried.

She turned and dived. Everybody dived and tried to swim underwater.

The plane came low. A German! It circled the lake. Everytime Catherine's head came up from the depths she was sure the plane was coming directly at her.

The nurses kept swimming and diving.

Now the Russian artillery opened. The gunners were not very good, but they were earnest. They peppered the sky with shrapnel, which fell into the water all around the swimming nurses.

Again and again the aviator circled the lake, apparently enjoying himself. At any moment, the girls thought, he might

drop a bomb, or fire his machine guns. It was impossible to
avoid him, swim as they would.

They quit swimming. They treaded water, collecting
together in a frightened group. The plane whished overhead,
circled, and once more started toward them. The shrapnel
followed its orbit.

The girls fled in a panic, swimming to the edge of the lake,
and fleeing down the road. The plane still circled around and
above them.

The girls stopped suddenly. There, on the wide porch of a
house at the edge of the village, were the officers of their
unit, one or two doubled up with laughter, one looking at
them through his field glasses.

They turned and ran the other way. They dived back into
the lake, no longer thinking of shrapnel or the circling plane.
They swam across the lake to the clump of trees, to the safety
of their clothes.

The German pilot soared back into the blue, the wings of
his plane shaking with laughter.

It was on this march to the front that Catherine de Hueck
was given a citation for bravery under fire.

It was shortly before noon, and it was either a Wednesday
or a Friday, for those were the only days on which fish soup
was served. On all other days there were chunks of meat in
the brew.

The commissary had taken possession of a little glade in a
forest. The soup was in a big kettle in the center of the opening, bubbling over a fire of pine logs. One of the cooks was
stirring it with a long wooden ladle. The bread was being
taken out of the ovens. The tea was nearly ready. The meal
would be served within a few minutes. Orderlies were lying
about on the grass or the black earth or the carpets of brown

pine needles. They were writing letters, mending harness or shoes, plunking on balalaikas, or sleeping peacefully.

And long lines of men were moving cautiously up through the trenches to get their noonday rations.

Without warning six German planes broke through a low gray cloud and circled about, looking for the Russian ammunition dumps. A fleet of Russian planes winged up to combat; and German and Russian artillerymen leaped to their guns.

Chunks of steel and iron rained on the camp.

The man with the soup ladle threw it away and scampered into the densest thicket. The letter writers, the sleepers, the musicians, the men mending leather, the cooks and orderlies and bakers, and the men in the trenches, gave way to panic.

In half a minute Nurse de Hueck was alone, and mad.

"Come back, you cowards!" she shouted. "Come back and eat."

Nobody paid the least attention to her.

She shouted the louder. She shouted in Russian, in English, in Arabic, in French, in Finnish and Ukrainian and Italian. She spiced her vocabulary of abuse with diabolic utterances she had overheard — words she had sometimes upbraided them for using.

"After all my work getting this meal ready for you," she shouted, "you are not going to run out on me."

One or two of the men, sheepish or ashamed, approached her.

To encourage the others she recovered the ladle, walked out into the open, and began to stir the still-bubbling soup.

More and more men began to show themselves. Some of them were laughing. Some of them were cheering.

And then — Plunk! — a great piece of shrapnel fell directly into the kettle. The soup went like a geyser up to heaven.

Nurse de Hueck stood where she was, not knowing what else to do. She was not hurt, though her right wrist was slightly burned. The soup was gone. The kettle was gone. But all the men were back; and they were roaring with laughter.

Catherine stared at them, wondering what was funny. Then she took note of her uniform. The soup had drenched it, and decorated it with the heads and the bones of many fish.

It was weeks later when the citation was given her.

It was just back of the front-line trenches, and a number of regiments were drawn up on parade, each line severely straight, every man standing rigidly at attention.

General Bastrokoff, himself, the chief of staff, stood on a little platform to inspect the heroes, to praise them, and to pin their decorations on them.

He was a short and stocky man. His head was clean shaven, like a Tartar's. His eyes were green and slanting. His legs were bowed with much service in the cavalry. And his face was stern, even when he smiled. He had made a reputation as a great soldier and a severe disciplinarian; and there wasn't a man in those thousands present who didn't respect and fear him.

The men whose names he called stepped out of ranks, advanced smartly to the platform, saluted stiffly, accepted the decoration and the kiss with countenances as set as wood, and marched back into line.

Nurse de Hueck, when her time came, went forward as smartly as the most bewhiskered veteran, saluted as punctiliously, and stood as solemn and as straight and as wooden as any of the men.

The general began to read the citation.

A man in the first rank, a few feet away, suddenly put his hand to his nose and made a sour face. The men next to him whispered to a comrade, and imitated the first. Down the line went a snicker, a holding of noses, and the whisper, "That's the heroine of the battle of Fish Soup."

The whisper and the snicker and the gesture swept through line after line of solemn men. It took possession of all the regiments. Not even the fear of Bastrokoff could prevail against so wonderful a joke.

Before the general was halfway through the citation several thousand men were roaring with homeric laughter.

The general's red face turned purple. His bristly scalp quivered. His green eyes blazed red with murder.

Catherine tried to whisper an explanation to him, but she could not make him hear. She had to shout. She had to shout as she shouted to the panic-stricken men in the glade.

"They laugh because I have already been decorated, sir," she shouted. "I was decorated by the Germans. With fish heads."

The general looked at her as he would at a crazy woman. He looked at his men. Some of them were shaking helplessly, crying real tears. Some had staggered out of line. Some were rolling on the ground in their crazy mirth.

"I stunk," Catherine shouted. "I stunk for days, no matter how often I washed my clothes."

"You stunk?" the general said.

"I stunk of fish soup, sir. Hot fish soup. With onions!"

"My God," the general said; and his laugh was heartier and louder than any of his heroes'.

He never finished reading the citation.

"Against these men," he said, when he had gained control of himself, "the enemy was helpless. You, a mere child, have made them helpless just by looking at them. Go with God."

3

LIFE, that had promised adventure and glory, provided constant danger, long marches, interrupted sleep, the noise of guns and planes, the groans and curses and screams of wounded men — and the duty of robbing the poor.

Once upon a time she had ministered to the poor, and envisioned herself as a nurse or a nun, spending her life in their service. With her mother she had visited their homes, had helped some old peasant woman with her wheat or hay, had brought fresh milk or butter or eggs from her father's farm to some sick old man, had helped to nurse some suffering little boy or girl.

Her mother had taught her how to treat a fever, how to dress a wound, had brought her up in the knowledge of herbs. Her mother's people had been doctors and surgeons for generations in Russia, and in England before they came to Russia.

Catherine had made up her mind to be a Red Cross nurse even before she became the bride of Baron Boris de Hueck. She had set out for the battle lines after he left to join his regiment of engineers. She had been sent back home and forced to enroll as a nurse's aid. She had been made to scrub floors, fetch and carry ill-smelling vessels, make bandages, and do a thousand other distasteful and monotonous tasks.

Now, part of her duty was to "requisition" the wheat, the oats, the hay, the wood, even the vegetables in the garden and the bread hidden in the house, of all the peasants near the camp. She must take from the poor everything they had, knowing they would perish.

"I'm sorry, Grandma," she had to say, "I know this is your last hen, and that its eggs keep you alive. But soldiers must be fed, though women die. And I must also take the fagots that keep you from freezing. The soldiers must be warm."

Why had she volunteered for duty at the front?

She began to realize that it was only because she was young. She began to realize, too, that she could never learn enough about nursing though she studied the rest of her life. She had been sent to the front not because she was a competent nurse, but only because there was such a woeful lack of nurses.

She spent sickening, wearying, dreadful hours in the medical tents. There were days and nights of piling up amputated arms and legs. Piling them up. Piling them up. Taking them from the operating tables or the blood-spattered floor, carrying them out, throwing them on the piles. Making new piles. Huge piles. Piles of torn arms. Sturdy young arms. Strong young legs. Limbs that had coaxed music out of wood and strings. Limbs that had danced and marched and run in panic or mad wrath.

Her uniforms reeked of blood and dirt and ether fumes. Her arms ached from the weight of the severed limbs. Her head sang with the prayers, the torture, the deliriums of dying men.

It was necessary for her to get away from it whenever she could, to visit some little canteen where she could look at men with two good arms and two whole legs, and think how wonderful it was to be alive and well. Or she would hurry into the woods, or to some wayside shrine, and pray for peace on earth and no more butchery among men.

She became inured to sleeping on the earth, wrapped in a

woolen cape. Black capes in summer, white in the winter snows. These capes were made of virgin wool. They had an abominable odor, but they were warm and almost impermeable to rain or dew.

She woke one night, dreaming that wild horses were leaping over her. She lay still and, looking up, saw horses' hoofs and bellies flying above her. She was not dreaming. A cavalry regiment was making a wild dash into some near-by battlefield.

She lay still.

The men could not see her because of her black cape. She might have been part of the black earth and nothing more. But the horses knew she was there, and she was confident none would step on her. She went back to sleep.

In October she fell asleep in the saddle, making a forced march, a retreat. It was raining. A cold rain. A steady downpour. Sometime after midnight the order was passed down the column to make camp. That was a bitter joke, she thought. Nobody could make fires in that rain, even if enough dry wood could be found; and it would be impossible to keep the fires burning if they could be started.

She unbuckled her camp bed from the saddle, placed it in as dry a spot as she could find in the dark, wrapped her cape around her, and went instantly to sleep. She woke to find herself in an ice cold stream. All of her, except her head, was immersed.

In the autumn months of 1916, there was bitter fighting in the marshes of White Russia, and the medical unit was short of supplies.

"We have no hay for the horses," an officer said, "and only a few days' supplies for the men. Get on your horse and ride to the quartermaster at X. Bring back everything you can."

X was a tiny camp about forty miles away. It was in territory that had been captured and recaptured half a dozen times. One of the Russian armies then occupied the area immediately west of X and immediately north. The area to the east and the south might, or might not, belong to the enemy.

The cavalcade left camp in the dark of the following morning. Forty huge drays. A man driving each one. Forty men and a sergeant. Nurse de Hueck led the way, riding her horse.

They went slowly, conserving the animals' strength. The poor beasts would have heavy work on the return trip. So it was not until late in the afternoon of the next day that they pulled into X, made a fire, and started the tea to boiling.

The young lieutenant in charge of the camp was, at first, too excited to talk.

"Go away," he said. "I can't give you anything. I've got nothing. Nothing but troubles."

"But I must have supplies for men and horses."

The officer cooled himself with a mouthful of vodka.

"Go away," he said again. "I can't be bothered with you. A mile away my comrades are dying of starvation, and I cannot help them. Only a mile away — and it might be a thousand for all I can do."

The men of whom he spoke, he explained finally, had been the advance of the army that chased the Germans across the river. They had gone too far. They were on a great spit of land, a triangle that jutted into the river, but they had to stay there.

"They are trapped," the officer said. "They are dead men even now."

The Germans, from across the stream, kept a curtain of shells and machine gun bullets falling on the base of the triangle. The men on the spit could not retreat without being annihilated. Neither could they advance, for the river was on three sides of them.

Catherine saw a narrow-gauge railroad track leading into the spit.

"Why can't you send supplies over that track?" she asked.

The officer handed her his field glasses.

"Take a look, lovely idiot," he said, "and answer that foolish question yourself."

Through the glasses she could see huge railroad engines lying on either side of the right of way, wrecked and burned; and great freight cars smashed and charred; and cabooses. And she could see, on the track and along its high banks, supplies of all kinds, and the bodies of many men.

"The Germans have the range," the officer explained. "They shell and machine-gun every train I try to send in there. Do you see now why I am going crazy?"

"Why don't you get some flatcars?" the nurse asked. "If the guns are set for targets as tall as freight cars, the shells will go over them; and the train will get by before the guns can find the right range."

"But they'd still hit the engine," the officer objected.

"Don't use an engine. Hitch a couple of horses on either side of the front car, whip them up and let them go. It's only a mile or so from here into that woods. The horses can make it all right."

The young lieutenant studied the beautiful nurse for a long time before he spoke.

"Now, why didn't I think of that?" he said then.

Catherine let her big eyes register nothing but girlish innocence.

"Sometimes," she observed, "God gives wisdom to the dumb which He denies to the intelligent."

Her father, she thought, the wily old diplomat, would be proud of that remark.

"At least we can load up one car," she went on. "I'll take it in."

The lieutenant shook his head.

"You don't want to die, so young, so charming, so clever?"

But before she could reply, he shrugged his shoulders.

"Well," he said, "there isn't anybody else. I have to stay here. I can't trust anybody. I guess I'll have to send you."

Catherine explained the situation to the forty-one men she had brought to X.

"We may be killed," she said, "but then our troubles are over. Or we may get through, and so we shall be able to help our comrades. I am asking for volunteers."

The forty-one men spoke as one. "I'll go."

"No. I want only ten."

She selected the escort. The flatcar was shunted onto the track. It was packed with bread, cocoa, tea, canned goods, hay, medicines, great chunks of meat, and such cigarettes as the lieutenant had. Bags of flour and sugar were stacked up around these and piled high as a sort of protection.

"The lieutenant will understand," Catherine said, "that I, as a Red Cross representative, cannot take any ammunition."

"The nurse will understand," the lieutenant replied, irritably, "that I have no ammunition to spare; that, in fact, I have no ammunition."

The nurse was not surprised. There was always a scarcity of ammunition, especially at the front.

The horses were hitched to the car. The nurse and the ten men climbed aboard, the drivers shoving bags of sugar and flour aside to make their tasks easier.

"Go with God," the lieutenant shouted. The drivers cracked

their whips. The horses strained. The car began to move, slowly, gradually gaining speed.

Catherine lay on her stomach, on cases of canned fish and beans, and said her prayers.

Cannons roared angrily. Machine guns chattered. Bullets ripped open the top bags of sugar and flour, and their contents fell on the escort like snow.

Faster and faster the horses ran, urged on by the cracking of whips, the thunder of the guns, and the whine and zing of bullets flying over their heads.

The distance to the woods was only a mile or so; a mile and a half at most; yet it seemed like twenty miles to the men and the girl.

The German fire ceased abruptly. The whips stopped cracking. The drivers called softly to the horses. The animals were no longer running, they were walking. Catherine looked up and saw trees.

And there were Russian soldiers all around the flatcar, shouting with joy, and giving thanks to God and all His saints.

A huge ruffian, an officer who hadn't shaved in weeks, picked up the nurse as she was climbing over the side, held her in his arms, and kissed the icing of flour and sugar off her face.

"That was the cleverest and most gallant thing I ever saw," he told her. "I'll see that you get the St. George Cross for this."

Catherine and the ten volunteers walked back in a ditch beside the track. It was dark, but the moon was shining. They saw the lieutenant pacing up and down before his little commissary shack. Catherine called to him. He turned, screamed, and reached for his gun. Then he laughed hysterically.

"I thought you were ghosts," he said. "I followed the flatcar, for a time, through the glasses. Suddenly it seemed to explode in a white cloud."

"The flour," Catherine explained.

"The flour!" The lieutenant looked chagrined. "Of course. Now, why didn't I think of that?"

The forty drays were fully loaded before morning, and started on their way — the drivers singing hymns. Catherine slept on her horse, and dreamed of the St. George Cross and of her father.

On a morning late in November she was awakened by the ringing of the telephone.

"Nurse de Hueck," she said sleepily.

"Nurse de Hueck," a man's voice repeated, the voice of the medical officer in command.

A regiment was marching toward a point about thirty miles to the northeast. There was a commissary post there, but nobody to take care of the men.

"Saddle immediately," the general said, "and gallop all the way."

Catherine knew the road she must take. It was narrow and treacherous. It wound through marshes. It was bordered in many places by quicksands and bogs. One must stay in the middle of that road. To get off it for an instant might mean death for horse and rider.

It was dark. Rain clouds had blotted out all stars. There was a wind that blew wet leaves against her face, so that, although she kept her flashlight burning, she could hardly see the path to the stables.

She untethered the horse, spoke to him gently, fed him a little sugar, thrust the flashlight into a pocket of her white cape, mounted, and started at a gallop down the road.

She had gone but a few miles when she fell asleep. She

woke in terror. Something had frightened the horse, and he was rearing and bucking. Before she could control the beast, the flapping of her white cape frightened him anew, and he pitched her over his head. As she struggled to rise, he stepped on her.

How long she lay in the road she could not tell. The rain beating on her face aroused her. She rested for a moment or two, then tried to find her flashlight. It had leaped out of her pocket when she fell, and perhaps it had landed in the quicksands.

She heard the animal breathing a few steps away. She managed to reach him, to soothe him. She stood a long time by his side, scarcely able to breathe, praying for strength. Somehow, she managed to get back into the saddle.

"Gallop," she said.

She had only strength enough to stay in the saddle. She couldn't guide the beast. She must trust to his instinct to find the right way, and to keep going.

She arrived at the commissary a little before dawn. She fell off the horse and lay unmoving. Blood was trickling from her mouth. She could not lift a hand to wipe it away. She could not talk.

She made signs to an orderly that she wanted to write a message. The soldier hurried away, returning with pencil and paper. She started to write instructions and fainted.

She stood up when a doctor arrived, but immediately collapsed at his feet.

It was not until days later that she knew what had happened. The pleura, the covering of her lungs, had been torn by the horse's hoofs, the doctor said. She must stay in bed for two weeks at least. And she must not worry. Everything would be done for her that could be done.

She was in the hospital when the decoration was presented to her — the medal of the Cross of St. George, the highest decoration a woman could hope to win. The cross itself was as highly prized in Russia as the Victoria Cross in England — but it had been awarded only posthumously to women.

She clutched the medal and its black and orange ribbon tightly in her hand. She had kept a promise made to her father.

Colonel de Kolyschkine had lamented that he was too old to take an active part in the war and that he could send no one in his place.

"This is a fight for freedom," he said, "and I must stay at home. It is intolerable. And I have no sons to give. Vsevolod still walks with a limp. His broken leg never entirely healed. And Serge and Andrew are only children. I will not win the St. George Cross again. And no son will win it for me."

"I'll be your son," Catherine had answered. "And I'll get you the cross — or the medal of the cross."

She was given permission to go home for the Christmas holidays. She sent her father a telegram, knowing it would never reach him, put on a new uniform, pinned the medal proudly to her tunic, and made her way to the stables. She was weak, but she felt able to ride a horse.

She went home slowly, for the roads were choked with deserters, with homeless and hungry and ill-clad peasants, with leaderless bands of robbers in uniform. It took her almost a week to reach the streets of Petrograd and the apartment where her family lived.

She paused a moment outside the door and remembered her father's words as though he had uttered them but an hour since. "Go with God, but never forget that if you disgrace your name or mine I shall come to you and kill you with my own hands, much as I love you. You are going into greater danger than you realize, danger to soul as well as body. Remember my honor and my words."

It was here she had knelt for his blessing.

She straightened up. It still hurt to breathe. But she summoned a smile to her lips, uttered a silent prayer, opened the door, and walked in like a soldier.

Her people were in the next room. She could hear them talking. It was almost time for dinner. She entered the room quietly and stood like a soldier at attention, trying not to cry.

They greeted her with a rush, with glad cries, with strong arms and fervent happy kisses. And they exclaimed at the medal shining on her tunic.

She put it into her father's hands.

"Thank you," was all he said.

He looked at her closely, ordered her to bed, and sent for a doctor.

*   *   *

"I'll never forget that entrance," Catherine said. "I guess there's something of the actress in me. I sure stopped the traffic that time!"

"I'll bet," Mr. Dee said. "Will you marry me?"

"Certainly not," she answered.

4

AT THIS time Petrograd was talking about the murder of Rasputin and prophesying the murder of holy Russia. The talk was linked with stories of graft and corruption in the imperial court, the defeats and disasters at the front, the death by starvation and exposure of millions of peasants, and the swarms of cutthroats and beggars in the city streets.

In all the tragic history of Russia there was no story equal, in Catherine's mind, to the slaying of the monk.

Rasputin had been one of the most powerful men in the empire. He claimed to be the only man who could cure the little Czarevitch, who bled too easily. Men said he used witchcraft or enlisted the aid of the devil. Others said he used herbs in ministering to the child. But all agreed that he exerted a baleful influence over the Czarina, and through her, over the government. Because of him and his hatred of Russia and love for Germany, men believed the Russian army was being destroyed. They pointed out that his friends, German ministers, had been appointed to conduct the war, that supplies were deliberately withheld from hard-pressed armies, and that hundreds of thousands of helpless Russians were thrown into battle unequipped even with rifles.

The men who murdered Rasputin, it became known, were not ordinary men. They were nobles, rich, respected. They were ardent patriots. They had felt it a duty to kill the man who had set out to kill Russia. And they had labored conscientiously for weeks to work out the method of assassination, and to perfect their plans in every detail.

They baited him with a woman, an exotic countess who existed only in the lying words of the conspirators. On the evening of December 16, they lured him to the spot where he was to die, by promising to introduce him to this woman. Women were Rasputin's weakness. He would go anywhere to meet one, if she was beautiful and rich.

The room to which he was led had been soundproofed and turned into a banquet hall in preparation for his coming. The table had been so arranged, or disarranged, as to make it appear that a number of men and women guests had been there, and had left but a moment or two ago — that the guest of honor might be alone with the countess.

"The countess," Rasputin was told, "has hurried upstairs to make herself as lovely as possible for your illustrious highness' sake. She is entertaining a few other ladies with American music."

One of the conspirators, listening in a room above, started a phonograph, playing "Yankee Doodle."

"She will come down as soon as she gets rid of her companions. Meantime — here are cakes and wine."

The pretty little cakes were loaded with deadly poison. The wine was mixed with instant death. Rasputin was not hungry. He was not thirsty.

The host excused himself in despair and hurried upstairs to his fellows. One of them had suffered such agonies of suspense that he had fainted.

"Make him eat," the others ordered. "Make him drink."

Rasputin ate and drank, eventually. He crunched the poisoned cookies greedily between his immense jaws, and gulped the wine. But he stayed in his chair and chatted calmly and demanded the countess come down.

"I'll fetch her," the host cried, eager to get upstairs.

"Poison will not kill him," he told his confederates. "He is the devil. He must be shot." He went downstairs with a small revolver and sent a bullet through Rasputin's chest. His friends came rushing into the room to find the monk lying on his back. There was a white bearskin rug under him, and a beautifully carved, ivory crucifix — a memento of Italy or Spain — looked down on him from the wall above. He was bleeding inwardly. The rug was not stained.

They moved him to the tiles near the fireplace, smoothed out the rug, effacing the imprint of his carcass, and hurried, each to his task, to prepare for the burial.

Half an hour later the man who shot the monk returned. He felt the wrist. There was no pulse. He put his palm against the heart. It did not beat. He raised up, and the dead man opened his eyes, and grasped the murderer's arm, and struggled to rise from the tiles.

The slayer screamed in abject terror, wrenched himself loose, and fled. Rasputin rushed after him, out of the house, into the snow. There another of the conspirators shot him twice, and killed him for the second time.

A little later they carried the body to the place selected and lowered it through a hole they had chopped in the ice of the river.

It was not so much the crime itself that nauseated and frightened Catherine — nor the fact that people swore an imperial grand duke had sanctioned the murder and taken part in it, a young man who some day might rule all the Russians.

It was the wave of jubilation that greeted the news, the

frenzied shouts of men celebrating a cowardly and carefully planned murder, and the foolish belief that now the Russian armies could turn a debacle into a decisive victory. And it was what people said about the phonograph that kept on playing "Yankee Doodle."

This was the song of revolution, they asserted, the song the young Americans had sung in the war with England. It was significant, that song. It was ushering in another revolution, the bloodiest the world should ever see.

They were right, the girl thought, but the revolution had begun before Rasputin ever left the safety of the imperial palace. She had seen it born of terror and famine and defeat, and of the lies of Communists. She had seen it tottering in blood and rags toward Petrograd, on her journey home.

But she held her peace.

Her family had worries enough. The doctor had told her she had contracted tuberculosis as a result of the horse's kick and her own disregard for herself on her weary ride from the front.

"We'll go to Antrea," her father said. "There are doctors there, too, perhaps more than I can find in Petrograd. And the winter air will help. We'll have Christmas there. You'll be strong and well again in no time."

The family owned eight hundred acres of farm land and forests at Antrea, in Finland — an estate not far from Viborg, and close to the River Voksa. There was a big house. There were horses and cows and sheep and chickens and turkeys and geese. There were many servants.

And there was a tree on a little hill where she had spent many hours of her girlhood dreaming.

She reveled in the life at Antrea, and forgot about her lungs. She even forgot about the murder of Rasputin and the talk of revolution. She plunged into the familiar work with zest. She walked miles through the woods looking for the right Christmas tree. She put on skis and went to the village stores. She helped with the work of getting the house ready for the great feast, scrubbing the floors, washing the woodwork, polishing the ikons until they shone, helping to bake the cake and make the gingerbreads.

Most of the servants had fled. Catherine was almost glad of that. It made so much more work for her, gave her so little time for fear.

The making of the gingerbreads engrossed her. They were cut in the shape of stars, in honor of the star that led the wise men to the crib, and in honor of our Lady, Star of the Sea. They were also cut in the image of the Child wrapped in swaddling clothes and laid in a manger. And they were cut in the shape of a lamb, in honor of the Lamb of God.

The biggest gingerbread, which was always a likeness of the good St. Nicholas, was decorated with gay colored ornaments, and was to be given to the child who had been the best during the year.

The family kept a rigid fast through Advent, and at dinner Catherine's father solemnly read the Epistles and Gospels of the day — and recited prayers as he lit the candles of the Advent wreath.

On Christmas eve the doors of a locked room were opened. And there was the tree with its tinsel and its synthetic snow and its lighted tapers, and the heaps of neatly tied and decorated packages under its green boughs!

Catherine rejoiced as the Christmas bells rang out, and she walked with her parents and her brothers through the glittering snow toward the church.

No matter what might happen, she thought, no matter whether she died of tuberculosis or bullet wounds or starvation, she would find her family again some day — and would remain forever and ever with them in the peace of the Infant God.

She talked but little to her father of the stories of impending disaster. He dismissed them with a few calm words.

"It is nonsense to think there will be a revolution, or that this great country will ever turn atheistic. That is the vaporing of weak and malicious minds.

"Are we not a devout and truly religious people? Are there not shrines to our Blessed Lady and to her crucified Son all over our holy land? How could we desert God and the lovely Bogoroditza — her who gave birth to God? If we do, then God will desert us. But that is a thought too horrible and ridiculous to contemplate."

Yet only a few days later Catherine, going into Petrograd for a checkup by her doctor, saw the beginning of the Kerensky revolution.

She had just left a coffee shop and was walking toward a hotel across the square, when a machine gun fired. People screamed and fled. Catherine fell, hugging the street. She didn't see who fired. She wasn't sure from what direction the shots came. She didn't wait to find out. She crawled across the square toward the revolving doors in the hotel lobby.

She arrived there safely, though her clothes were soiled and torn. The police came. They asked a few questions and went away. Nobody knew what had happened, nor why. Nobody asked how many men and women had been killed or wounded, nor who they might be.

The doctor pretended not to have heard of the shooting. He made a quick examination.

"Yes," he said. "It is certainly tuberculosis. You must go to a sanitarium. There is a place in Finland. . . ."

He was silent for a moment. He lowered his voice.

"I envy you, Nurse de Hueck. You will be far away."

The sanitarium was not a great distance from Antrea; but Catherine stayed there only a few days. There was a shortage of doctors and nurses. The food was scanty and very bad. She felt worse than when she arrived.

"My mother is a nurse," she told the authorities, "and she has food, the sort of food I need. I am going home."

* * *

"My father was doing the plowing when I came home," Catherine said. "There was only one man servant left on the place, and he was too old to be of any help. The others had run off to the armies — or joined the Communists.

"I went to work, cutting potatoes and planting them. I planted five acres of potatoes, Mr. Dee — and thought my back would break."

Mr. Dee, whose name really wasn't Dee, said nothing.

"I milked the cows, too. Thirty-six of them. And made cheese and butter. That butter was worth something like twenty dollars a pound. Mother sold it, but not for money, of course. Nobody had any money, and money didn't mean anything anyway. It had no value. She might get fifty cabbage seedlings for a few pounds of butter, or maybe a pair of old shoes. We had given away so much clothing and so much food, we were in pretty desperate straits.

"I did a man's work on the farm, and I did a woman's work too. Sometimes, when mother was out bargaining for food or clothing, I even cooked the dinner."

"You can cook?" Mr. Dee exclaimed. "When are you going to marry me?"

"Never, Mr. Dee, thank you," she said. "And don't ask me that again."

✺ 5 ✺

IT IS impossible to say, with accuracy, that Catherine was fifteen or sixteen when she first went to war. She was born, while traveling with her mother to the fair at Nijni-Novgorod, in a Pullman car a few miles outside that city.

The day was August 15, and the year was either 1899 or 1900. Catherine's mother was ill for a number of years thereafter, and never remembered the year. If there are records left undestroyed by the Communists, they are unavailable.

But she believes the year was 1900.

Her mother's maiden name was Emma Thompson. She was of English and French descent. One of her ancestors was the celebrated painter, Vernee. Another was the first English physician invited to Russia by the Czar. Nicholas I brought him to Petrograd to open the first official hospital in Russia, early in the eighteenth century.

Her father's people, the De Kolyschkines, had been in Russia for nine centuries. They were landed gentry, and had produced many soldiers, diplomats, farmers, businessmen, priests, and bishops.

Her father, Theodore, had begun his career as a lieutenant in the army; but after the disgrace of his father, Archip, he had gone into business. Eventually he became a member of the board of directors of a big insurance company. He traveled all over the world as its commercial representative, and at the same time, unofficially, he served as a diplomat.

Archip seems to have been a nice old man. When he retired from active military life, because of wounds suffered in the Crimean War, Alexander II gave him many honors and estates, and placed him in charge of the polit bureau.

One of the political prisoners asked permission to go to Switzerland, where his wife was dying. He wanted to look upon "the only face in the world that is dear to me," before it was changed by death. Then, the man swore, he would return to prison immediately. Archip was no fool. He investigated the prisoner's story and found he had a wife and that she was dying. He made the husband swear a most solemn oath, and let him go. The man never came back.

The Czar confiscated Archip's estates, exiled him, and placed a black mark against his name in the imperial archives.

These were the circumstances that impelled Theodore to resign his commission in the Grodno Hussars. It cost a small fortune to maintain oneself as an officer in the Russia of that time. He came back into the army in 1885, when Russia went to war with Turkey over the liberation of Bulgaria.

He obtained a commission in a regiment of the line, and managed to see plenty of fighting. And several times, evidently, he was seen in battle by Alexander III.

The war did not last long. Shortly after it was ended, the lieutenant made an expedition into the Caucasus. An ambush had been prepared by the wild tribesmen, and part of the detachment rode into it. De Kolyschkine, by his recklessness — and a mad charge into the thick of the ambushers — managed to save the general. He was wounded in the head — and recommended for the St. George Cross.

He appeared before the Czar, wearing some of the highest decorations in the gift of the emperor; and Alexander studied him for wordless seconds.

He was a lion of a man. He stood about six feet, four inches, and was built like a granite statue. The Czar looked at his face, at the medals on his tunic, at the bloodstained plumes that covered the imperial eagle on his helmet, at his military bearing.

"We have seen you in action," he said. "You are an officer no one could forget. What is your name?"

"My name, sire, is De Kolyschkine."

"You are not the son of that De Kolyschkine the revered Alexander II banished for neglect of duty?"

"The same, sire. But, if I might presume on your imperial majesty's kindness, I should like to say it was my father's belief in human nature that was at fault, never his loyalty to the Czar."

Alexander seemed to like that. He waved his fairy wand; and all was right again with the house of Kolyschkine.

The young officer had been made colonel of his old regiment, the Grodno Hussars, and was 34 when he met Emma Thompson. His first wife had died in giving birth to his son, Vsevolod; and the boy was 13 years old when his father married for the second time.

Miss Thompson had been graduated from the Imperial Conservatory of Music in St. Petersburg, and might have been a great pianist, had she wished to be. She might also have become a doctor or a nurse. She had learned considerable about medicine from her father — the product of generations of English physicians and surgeons — and she had acquired a great knowledge of herbs.

But her ambition was "going to the people," to use a Russian idiom. She worked as a telephone operator in Petrograd, principally that she might teach the catechism to her sister workers. She toiled as a domestic on various farms, helping the old people with the crops and the young with their lessons. She was a little bit of a woman and seemingly fragile; but she could pitch hay with the huskiest of men.

"It seems ironic," Catherine says, "that a woman who could play the piano so well, who was so deeply devoted to music, should marry a man who had no ear at all for music. But she made the best of it."

Natalie, the first child born to Colonel de Kolyschkine and his second wife, died shortly after birth. So did the next two babies.

The fourth child was a husky baby, and when the mother was sure it would live, she determined to give her the name Catherine — in honor of her husband's first wife. She may have been jealous of that unfortunate young woman; but she never let her husband know of it.

The colonel's wife was perhaps the only person who had no awe of him. She was sweet and gentle, yet she could manage him with a look or a word.

The colonel was stern. In the discipline with which he ruled the family he was rigid. Yet the children adored him. When he wasn't at home to take them for their usual Sunday walk through the park, they were desolate. They were afraid to displease him. They never failed to say "sir" to him. Yet, every night before they went to bed, they ran to him, kissed his hand, and asked his blessing.

He was an odd mixture of strength and weaknesses. English and French diplomats called him "the Russian bear" or "the giant fox," and watched him wherever he went. The poor came to him for help. The rich and powerful came to him for advice. He had a huge contempt for money, yet usually had more than he knew what to do with. After he died, members of the family learned for the first time that he had helped 250 young people through college, and expended fortunes in other charities.

He was an epicure. He delighted in making certain sauces. He was a connoisseur of wine. He was a fop, a dandy. He had his clothes made in Saville Row, London; and there wasn't a suit in his wardrobe that had cost him less than thirty guineas. These were, of course, in addition to his uniforms, and the buckskin pants he wore when he attended the dowager empress. Those pants had to be soaked overnight. They were put on wet, to dry on the skin. Thus they were skintight.

He had his own barbers, manicurists, pedicurists, and valets. He changed clothes four times a day. He rose early in the morning, took a cold bath, and went for a ride or a walk. He ate a tremendous breakfast, then went to his office. Dinner was always at 6, and everybody was expected to be punctual.

He was an exquisite swordsman, an expert shot with rifle or pistol, and an excellent drinking man.

"He used to talk, sometimes, about a drinking bout in Ireland," Catherine remembers. "There had been an international competition between cavalry officers in Dublin. When it ended the contestants competed with the bottle. First, the South Americans went under the table, then the Latins, then the Germans and the British. Finally there were only three men drinking, Father and two Irishmen. Then, he confessed with some chagrin, he left one of the Irishmen sitting upright and drinking them down, and went to join his comrades under the tables."

Reverses never bothered him. One night at dinner he gave his wife a diamond pendant and a smile.

"This is the last bauble for a long time, Minia" — his pet name for her — "maybe a very long time. We've lost all our money. The Lord giveth. The Lord taketh away. Blessed be the name of the Lord. Dismiss the servants tomorrow. Give them each a month's wages. And look for a small flat."

He had invested heavily in a shipment of cotton to the United States. It had been stored, temporarily, in San Francisco, and was destroyed in the fire that followed the earthquake in 1906.

"I thought it great fun to be poor," Catherine says. "We got a little flat. We all pitched in to do the work. We had only one servant, a slovenly, goodhearted woman who urged us on at our tasks. I thought we were going to stay ruined, but when I asked Father about it he said no, we were only half-ruined. A little later he said we were not ruined at all; and we took a whole floor on the nicest street in Petrograd, and hired fourteen servants."

This new home became a rendezvous for all sorts of people, especially drunks. De Kolyschkine had a weakness for these people. The more hopeless they were, the more fond of them he seemed. He brought them home, cleaned them, clothed them, fed them, and sent them to institutions for a rest and a cure. Later he got them jobs.

Every so often there was a big dinner party in this flat, with an orchestra playing, and scores of guests. Catherine recalls there was at least one American millionaire who attended such a party. De Kolyschkine announced his advent with something of a flourish.

"Get out your best china, Minia. Mr. J. P. Morgan of New York is coming to dinner this evening."

The little woman looked up. "Haven't I heard that name before?"

"Of course. He's a multimillionaire. His name is known all over the world."

"What does he do?"

The colonel shook his head, signifying he didn't know what Morgan did, outside of banking.

"Does he know anything about music, for instance, or literature, or painting?"

The colonel looked gloomy. "No. I cannot conceive his knowing anything about art, even his own old masters, nor about music, nor anything except finance."

"He will probably be a dreadful bore," the wife concluded. "I shall give him my second-best china."

De Kolyschkine, says Catherine, had a great charm for all sorts of people, especially women. Wherever he was, women flirted with him; and he flirted mildly with them. He said the nice things they expected, at the right time; yet he always let it be known he regarded his wife as the queen of all women.

There was nothing petty about him, even in his religious beliefs and observances; yet his daughter once saw him in such a terrible rage that she quaked with fright.

A friend had made some remark about the Eastern rite custom of serving Holy Communion under both species, the priest giving a spoonful of Wine with a morsel of Bread to each communicant. The man thought this practice "unhygienic."

"Suppose," he said, "that some syphilitic should take Communion just before you. . . ."

A great wind blasted him before he could say another word.

"I'd not hesitate. And neither should you."

Anger all but twisted the colonel's face out of its usual dignity. He shot up from the table until he seemed eight feet tall, and glowered at his hapless friend.

"Don't you realize the Body and Blood of our Lord is healing?" he thundered. "How dare you express such impious thoughts?"

He did not practice the Russian Orthodox Catholic religion of his paternal ancestors. His was the "Religion of Rome," which came through his mother, Pani Maria Lisetzka, the Polish girl who ran away from her home in Warsaw to marry the handsome Archip.

6

CATHERINE traveled all over Europe and Asia with her parents, even when she was an infant. But her earliest recollections are not of trains or ships or sedan chairs. Nor of camels. They go back to her childhood in Egypt, and to a beautiful villa in Ramleh, a suburb of Alexandria.

A few incidents stand out.

She was swimming. The surf threw her, and she gashed her knee against a sharp rock. Her father took her out into deep water for the curative effect of the brine, and told her that Russian officers' little girls never cried.

"Child," he said, "you must learn never to weep because of physical pain, thus schooling yourself for the spiritual pain that comes inevitably to every Christian.

"You must have courage. You must fight. Fight always. Stand with your back against a wall so you can see your enemies face to face. Die, but do not ever surrender. Die fighting."

She didn't cry. Nor did she cry when she thought she was going to die of amoebic dysentery. She had bitten into a tangerine plucked from the garden, not knowing that all fruit must be boiled in Egypt. She went to bed deathly ill.

"Don't cry, Father," she said. "I'm going to be a little angel. It ought to be fun to fly around with the other angels, don't you think?"

The Russian bear wept.

44

He had brought doctors from Athens, Paris, London, Budapest, and other cities across the Mediterranean, but none of them had helped.

This disease travels upward from the feet, making the body cold. When the chill reaches the heart the patient dies.

Catherine was cold and lifeless from her feet to her waist when her father learned of an English doctor who had "gone native."

"He is a magic doctor," an Arab servant said, "but always drunk, and unreliable at best."

The colonel hunted up the man, kidnaped him from his harem, washed him, sobered him, and propelled him into the sickroom. The doctor prescribed a simple remedy, to be taken orally. Seeds of pomegranate steeped in alcohol for twenty-four hours in the tropic sun. The concoction worked "like magic."

Catherine was five or six, then, and a student in the convent school conducted by the Ladies of Zion — who today conduct similar schools in Kansas City, and in Moosejaw, Canada.

She spoke Arabic as fluently as Russian, for she used to play with the children of a Bedouin encampment near the villa.

"I picked up other things than the language," she recalls, "notably a certain dance. It looked so beautiful when the women performed it under the stars and the moon that I could scarcely wait until I exhibited it to my parents.

"Unfortunately, I chose the wrong time, for the house was filled with guests. They were not at all pleased. Rather, they were horribly shocked. They said it was the most vulgar dance they had ever seen, and I was sent to bed in disgrace."

She learned modern Greek, Italian, French, German, and English in these early days; and before she was twelve, could also speak Finnish, Ukrainian, Polish, Serbian, and Bulgarian.

And, not only in the convent school but also in her father's house, she learned the principles of her religion.

The Lenten observances and the Easter celebration especially impressed her.

The family prepared for the great day by a rigorous fast. The colonel read the Gospels and Epistles of the day, or spoke on religious topics at dinner. On the day before he went to confession, he fasted austerely, spent half a day before the Blessed Sacrament, and made a microscopic examination of his conscience.

The next morning, before he went to church, he called all the family together, the servants, the governess, and the tutors. To each he made a grave bow; and to each he spoke in the age-old formula of the Eastern rite:

"In the name of Christ, forgive me if I have offended or scandalized you."

Each in turn answered, "May God forgive you as I do," and then kissed him on the cheek, three times in honor of the Holy Trinity.

During Holy Week the women busied themselves with the making of *koolich* — the Easter bread, and the *pas-ha* — a mixture of cottage cheese, butter, eggs, sugar, and raisins, molded in wooden molds so that it contained the symbols of the opening of the tomb, and the words, "Christ is risen; verily He is risen."

The koolich might have many shapes, but some would be round, signifying infinity which has no end. The eggs, symbol of life and of fertility in Christ, would be colored yellow, for spiritual wealth; green for spring and for hope; or white, for charity, for purity, and for faith.

Toward midnight on Holy Saturday the family gathered for Mass. The colonel would take the bread, his wife the pas-ha, or "pasch," and the children the eggs. These would be placed on the altar steps to be blessed. Some would be taken home, some left for the poor.

At the Mass, after the priest had cried out in a loud voice that Christ had risen, and the congregation had answered, "Verily, He has risen," the priest kissed the deacon; the latter kissed the subdeacon; and everybody in the church turned and gave the kiss of peace to his neighbor. Then all the bells began to peal as they had not pealed throughout the year.

There were presents at the house, just as at Christmas; and relatives and friends visited the villa all day to give the kiss of peace — especially to little blonde Catherine.

Easter was the greatest feast of the year to the Russians, a day of extreme joy; just as Lent was always the most mournful season.

"Lent was mournful," Catherine says, "but it was also a time of feverish cleaning, dusting, and scrubbing, a period in which we got everything, inside and outside us, immaculate and ready to meet the risen Christ. Our souls shone like the ikons."

One Easter time, when Catherine was six or seven, the Kolyschkines made a pilgrimage to the Holy Land, visiting Nazareth, Bethlehem, the Garden of Olives, the hill of Calvary, and other places that knew the Son of God.

Two footprints on a rock attracted the attention of the child.

"That is where Jesus stood when He ascended into heaven," the guide told her. "You can still see the full print of His right foot, but only the toes of the left."

"But why have they put up a rope?" Catherine asked.

"This is a holy place," the guide explained. "The rope is to keep the pilgrims back, so that they will not profane the footprints. Otherwise, everybody who came here would want to stand where the Son of Man once stood."

Catherine was tempted beyond her strength. She wormed her way through the crowd until she was just outside the rope. Then she slipped under it, placed her tiny feet carefully in the big prints, and stood in prayer for a long blessed moment.

Half a dozen priests and nuns cried out, as though they had witnessed sacrilege, and many women began to scold the little girl. An old Franciscan priest calmed them.

"Suffer little children to come unto Me," he quoted, "of such is the kingdom of heaven."

Sometimes, during the pilgrimage, Catherine was sure she was going to die of reverence and awe. This was especially so in Nazareth. As she watched the women in their bright colored robes washing their clothes by the well, or beating them against the stones, or carrying jars of water on head or shoulder, or cleaning the clay floors of their little houses — wetting the clay with tepid water and then leveling it with a board and erasing all the tiny footsteps — she felt that at any moment she might meet the Blessed Virgin!

Ever since those days she has pictured the Mother of God as one of those beautiful Jewish girls, dark, graceful, with vivid red hair and big, black eyes.

She spent several hours in the Garden of Olives, where the Lord shed tears of blood, wondering if those gnarled, grotesque, enormous trees were not the very ones that saw His agony.

Her father was given a bottle of olive oil pressed from the fruit of those trees. And with it, years later, Catherine is sure, he performed a miraculous cure.

"It was during the year of the cholera epidemic in Russia, she says, "Mother was dying, or so the doctor thought. She had turned blue. The physician had left the house, and had gone to obtain a burial permit.

"Father remembered the olive oil and anointed Mother with it. I came into the room as he was rubbing it on her arm. He was praying. I could hardly believe what I saw. The oil seemed to remove the blue from the flesh, as though it were wiping off a dye, and to restore the natural color.

"When the doctor came back with the permit filled out for her burial, Mother had got out of bed and was drinking a little broth."

Catherine's sojourn in Egypt ended abruptly when an Arab sheik fell in love with her, and asked her hand in marriage.

Colonel de Kolyschkine could neither speak nor understand Arabic. The sheik could converse in no other language. Therefore Catherine was called in as an interpreter.

At first, she was merely puzzled. The sheik was so flowery she didn't know what he meant.

"Most illustrious of men, I have found a pearl of great price that is now in your most fortunate keeping; a pearl that dances; that dances in and out of my harem. I have seen this pearl many times among my women, and my heart desires her.

"I have diamonds, rubies, sapphires, opals, baubles not worth considering in the light of this pearl's serene gold beauty. I shall give you her weight in them, if you choose. Or, if your mind is on rare silks and satins and fine linens, I can fill a storehouse with them. The most exquisite patterns, the daintiest textures, the most durable qualities."

The colonel was icily polite as his daughter translated. He bowed to the sheik. His face showed profound respect.

"Tell the man," he bade her, "that my house is deeply honored at this mark of his esteem and friendship, and say that my little one is unworthy of the supreme honor he extends to her."

Suddenly Catherine understood.

She put the words into Arabic.

"Now say that my golden pearl is an empty-headed child and that I am sending her to Paris, where she may receive the training that will make her more suitable for so noble a husband."

Catherine rebelled.

"I won't marry him," she said. "I won't. I won't, sir. Please don't make me say I will."

"Be quiet," her father commanded sternly, "and repeat to him exactly what I have said."

Catherine obeyed, but with a mental reservation.

"Now tell him this. 'When this unworthy one becomes your bride she will be even as her older sister, Natalie.'"

"But Natalie is dead," Catherine objected.

"Exactly," her father said. "Now repeat the words 'When this unworthy . . .'"

Catherine spoke as gravely as her father did.

The sheik bowed low.

"One thing more," her father added. "Say, 'it is a great pity, mighty sheik, that you have never met my daughter, Natalie; but I hope you will see her soon.'"

After the sheik withdrew Catherine looked at her father and knew why people thought him both a fox and a bear.

"We must get you out of Egypt at once," he said, "otherwise you may be kidnaped. If that happens you would never see any of us again. Once locked in a harem there would be no escape; for it is unlawful, even for a minister of the czar, to invade the sacred precincts of any man's harem."

She was put on the first boat out of Alexandria, destination France; and was enrolled in the Lycee Mlle. Milliard in Paris.

7

CATHERINE'S parents had many servants, but they thought it wise that the girl should learn to do everything they did. The mother believed every woman should know how to cook, bake bread, weave, knit, sew, nurse, milk, make butter and cheese, put up preserves, and do everything else she might someday be forced to do.

At Antrea they had many sheep. So the women made woolen clothes. They had acres of flax. So they made linens.

Catherine worked at many "trades." She might be released from the task of helping the cook or the waitress or the seamstress, to go and weed a neighbor's garden. Or she might be asked to row across the river or to ski three or four miles on an errand. If she did less than eighteen miles a day on skis during the winter, she says, she thought it was a holiday.

The weaving was done in a big workroom, an airy, sweet-smelling place, with thousands of aromatic herbs hanging from the rafters.

"We would wet the linen," she says, "and the sun would dry it. The cloth was a gray-yellow when it came from the looms. We put it out on the March snow. The sun is especially fierce in March in this part of Finland.

"At night the cloth would freeze. In the morning it would thaw. Maybe rain would fall. That didn't matter. The linen stayed outdoors for weeks until it was as white as the snow on which it rested, and as beautiful. That linen would wear for generations."

Now and then Mme. Kolyschkine called a halt to all other duties, and went into the fields for herbs, or took Catherine into some poor village near by, visiting the homes of the sick and tending those most in need.

Occasionally they went on a pilgrimage. They would put on simple linen robes, and carry brown woolen capes such as St. Francis might have worn. They would fasten ropes about their waists for cinctures, and start out, barefooted, to walk two hundred miles or more to some famous shrine. Sometimes scores of others accompanied them.

They carried a little food, a loaf of black bread, a small package of salt, and a flask or bottle of water. At noon they would pause on the road, eat the bread and salt, wash it down with a little water, rest for an hour rolled up in their capes, and then push on. They might travel anywhere from twelve to eighteen miles a day.

The men in the party would go first, in a long line, where the road was narrow; and the women would follow. When there was room enough for two columns, men and women traveled side by side, saying litanies and other prayers or chanting the psalms.

At evening they usually stopped at a village. Then they would go, singly or in pairs, to knock at doors and beg shelter. "We are pilgrims going to a holy place," was the usual greeting. "God's peace to this house." The answer was always the same. "And God's peace to you, holy pilgrims." Food and shelter were never refused.

Sometimes the pilgrims slept in a hayloft. Sometimes they were given places over the oven. The Russian oven always takes up a great part of the kitchen. It has a flat top. The floor of the sleeping room, which is reached by a few steps up from the kitchen, is actually the covered ceiling of the oven.

Shortly after Catherine came to New York, some friends suggested a pilgrimage to the Jesuit Martyrs' shrine at Auriesville, N. Y. There would be a long holiday over the week end; and Catherine decided to go. She looked at the map with some concern, but assured herself that if those frail-looking girls could walk there and back in a few days, so could she.

It occurred to her that her friends would not go barefooted, since, even at Coney Island, American women were reluctant to show their naked feet. They wore slippers or sandals of a sort into the surf.

She put on heavy hiking shoes, packed a few loaves of black bread in a bag, put in some salt and a bottle of water, snatched up a heavy coat, and walked to the address on 42nd Street, where the pilgrims were to assemble.

All the other girls were in light summer things, and wore high-heeled shoes. They were going to Auriesville "American style" — on a bus!

Two brothers followed Catherine into the family. Serge came seven years after her, and Andrew took another seven to make his appearance.

"I suppose they were ordinary boys to everyone but me," Catherine declares, "but I adored them. I actually venerated Vsevolod. He was so much older. Serge, from the time he was old enough to talk until I was married, was my constant companion; and Andrew was, of course, the most wonderful baby ever born."

Her brothers shared her awe and love of her father. Even Vsevolod was afraid to approach the colonel when he needed extra spending money. Like Serge, he always sent Catherine to ask for it.

And, undoubtedly, the boys learned as much Christianity from their father as did Catherine.

Serge was bouncing a rubber ball outside the country house one autumn afternoon, when an old lady came by and begged for an alms.

"Sorry," Serge said, counting as he bounced, "twenty, twenty-one, twenty-two, twenty-three. Not today, Grandma. Twenty-four, twenty-five, twenty-six. Come tomorrow."

His father summoned him and asked what the old lady had wanted. Serge, no longer interested in the bouncing ball, told the story without trying to justify himself.

"You haven't sent away a poor old woman," his father said. "You have sent away Christ Himself — for, whatsoever you have done to one of His poor you have done unto Him. How would you like it, when you finally reach the judgment day, if Christ should say, 'Not today, Serge; come tomorrow'?"

Serge hung his head.

"I wouldn't like it, sir."

"No, you wouldn't. In eternity, as on this earth, there is no tomorrow. You would never more see the face of Mercy. Now go find that old lady, and do all a good Christian should do for her."

Catherine loved that country place at Antrea — about two hours by train from Petrograd — better than any other place on earth; for there was a hill there with a great tree on its summit, which had become a sort of shrine for her dreams.

"I always felt close to God in the country," she says, "and closer still when I lay under that tree on the hill, and let myself imagine my future life. Sometimes I would be a nun in some far-off cloister; sometimes a medical missionary in the jungles. Sometimes I would be a wife of some good man, living in a house beside the sea or high above some rushing river. And I would have a dozen children."

She dreamed there, during the spring and summer months,

when not busy studying, hiking, riding a horse, rowing, swimming, working in the house or the fields, or practicing her tennis.

She had left the Paris school and entered the Princess Obolensky High School in Petrograd, and had become something of a tennis champion. She represented the Imperial Russian Tennis Association in the junior doubles, during a number of international tournaments.

"We lost to the English," she says, "and we liked them. We beat the Germans, and they hated us."

The war was coming, and national loves and hates had heightened.

In the summer of that year, 1914, Catherine was standing, barelegged, on a ladder placed against a cherry tree on the rim of the orchard. Her mind was on tennis, not on cherries.

Suddenly she saw her father. He had just come from the city, and evidently he had good news of some kind. She hurried down the ladder and ran to meet him, carrying a basket of ripe cherries.

"Child," he said, "I have arranged a marriage for you."

In her excitement the girl almost stepped into the cherries.

She was only fourteen. But she was tall. She had come to maturity early in the hot sun of Egypt. She looked much older than her years. And many people regarded her as a "full-grown woman."

She did not ask the name of the man who was to be her husband. She was too amazed at the news to realize, at first, its full implication. Maybe, she thought, she had misunderstood. It might be some relative for whom the colonel had arranged a marriage.

But he continued, "You and Boris will solemnize your engagement on your birthday, August 15."

As soon as she could, Catherine hurried away to the tree upon the hill.

Boris. Her first cousin. The son of the old Baron Guido de Hueck, and of Aunt Vera, her father's sister. He was in his thirties, an officer in a regiment of engineers, and the only one of her relatives who had ever told her she was beautiful.

She neither liked nor disliked him. She was aware that he liked her. She remembered that he had paid her many compliments. And that was strange. Her mother had always told her she was a plain little girl, and should thank God He had given her intelligence, though He had denied her any sort of beauty.

Catherine thought it would be nice to be married. She would have money of her own. She could buy herself all the candy she could eat. She could gorge herself on caviar. She could buy all the pretty clothes she wanted. She could travel all over the world. And she could give lots of money to the poor.

She hurried from the hill to her bedroom, got out all her dolls, arranged them in a long row, and told them the news.

Russia and Germany were at war when the priest came to solemnize the engagement. But Boris' regiment was still stationed in Petrograd; and nobody thought of danger. Russia had fought many wars; and the wars always ended. What had war to do with marriages or engagements?

There were many parties in the big flat in the city. All the girl friends of the bride-to-be came to congratulate her, and to wish her well. There were sessions with dressmakers, appointments with the makers of underthings, with hairdressers, with manicurists and milliners and boot- and shoemakers. There were letters and telegrams, visits from relatives.

There was as much cleaning and scrubbing of the house and

Catherine with her parents, Theeodor and
Emma Kolychkine During Their Stay in Egypt

The Family Apartment in St. Petersburg in 1908
— It Took the Entire 3rd floor

The cottage in Finland: Here they were first starved by Red Soldiers then liberated by counter revolutionaries

Baron and Baroness de Hueck on board the Norwegian fishing smack that took them from Communist Russia

as much polishing of the ikons as there had been at Easter. And, most exciting of all, there were hundreds and hundreds of presents — mysterious packages the bride-elect could not wait to open.

And there were family conferences.

Her mother's brother, Constantine; and her mother's sisters, Eugenie, Charlotte, and Olga; and her father's sisters, Mary, Olga, and Vera — these and others instructed her in many things. How to conduct herself as a baroness. At court. In society. In the homes of peasants. At a banquet or a ball or in a box at the opera. How to run a large house economically. How to get work out of lazy servants.

Aunt Vera told her all about the baron's likes and dislikes in food and wine, women's clothes, women's jewelry, in the way a woman arranged her hair. Boris, she said, like any other European husband of consequence, would go shopping with her to see that she took only the right gowns and cloaks and hats, bought the right perfumes, selected the correct adornments. He would accompany her even when she bought shoes, hose, handkerchiefs, or underwear.

"And you must always be guided by his choice."

On the morning of her wedding day, the colonel came into his daughter's room. She had put on the beautiful white satin dress, and the maids were arranging the veil.

De Kolyschkine looked at his daughter a long time, speechless. Then he bade her to turn around.

"You are very beautiful," he said.

And there were tears in his eyes.

She thought then that he wept because he was going to lose her. But the years brought her another idea.

He had believed that this was the best marriage that could possibly be arranged for his much-loved child. It would give her riches and social prestige. The De Huecks had been nobles for centuries in Russia. They had been nobles in Holland before Peter the Great brought them to Russia to build his ships. The family owned many cotton mills; and Boris' father was one of the few "cash millionaires" in Russia. There were many who were millionaires in lands, houses, or goods; but Guido was rich in goods and in cash.

He had built his daughter's future on a rock. Or so he thought. Now, studying her in her bridal finery, it seemed to him, perhaps, that he had built that future on the sands of a girl's immaturity.

They were married in a private chapel in St. Isaac's parish in Petrograd, on January 25, 1915, with all the pomp and splendor of the ritual; then returned to the Kolyschkine flat to taste of bread and salt.

"Bread is, or was, not only the principal food of Russia, but a symbol of many things," Catherine said. "Did not the Son of God turn bread into His own Body? And is there a Christian in Russia today who will not pick up a piece of bread on the sidewalk or the street and place it where it will not be trodden upon — and who will not then bless himself before he continues on his way?

"At the home of the bride's parents, immediately after the ceremony in the church, the married pair were presented with a loaf of bread held on a wooden tray. Usually the bride's father held out the tray to them. In this instance the bread was a symbol of material goods, the stuff of the earth.

"The salt was offered by the bride's mother, and had a spiritual significance.

"'Ye are the salt of the earth. But if the salt lose its savor . . .'"

As soon as she could get away from her relatives and friends the bride packed all her dolls. She was not going to leave them home alone while she went on a honeymoon. And, at the first opportunity, she bought herself a five-pound box of candy.

On the honeymoon trip to Riga, Latvia, she ate every bit of the candy. It made her sick.

In Riga, Boris gave a party for all his relatives, and the bride acted as hostess for the first time in her life — and suffered her first great humiliation.

One of the most unbending of her husband's relatives accidentally intruded into Catherine's bedroom and discovered the dolls. She brought them down — all she could carry in her arms — to show the family what a silly child Boris had taken for a wife.

Nothing could have infuriated Boris more than this. He had always been angered when his wife's tender years were talked of.

Yet whenever he appeared with her in public some old friend was sure to hurry up with some such greeting as, "Why, Boris, I didn't know you had a daughter; and such a beautiful little girl!"

He was angry, too, because Catherine acted like a child, saying "yes, sir" to him, and "thank you, sir," as though he were old enough to be her father.

Catherine snatched up her dolls and hurried from the room — wishing she had that tree on the hill to fly to and its rough friendly bark to wet with her salt tears.

o   o   o

"I'll build you a house on a river," Mr. Dee said gently. "And as for the twelve children . . ."

"For land's sake shut your mouth," the baroness whispered fiercely. "There are people all around us. And I wouldn't marry you, Irishman, even if I could."

8

THE second time Nurse de Hueck went to war, life spoke to her in terms of horror. It was in April of 1917. An order from the Red Cross was forwarded to her at Antrea. She was still tubercular; but she decided to obey the order. Nurses were so badly needed.

Her father nodded his head when he read the order.

"You can die only once," he said.

He handed her a small revolver, a pearl-handled weapon. She stuck it in the top of her right boot, and asked his blessing.

"Go with God," he said. "I hope you never have occasion to use the weapon. But, if you do — shoot straight."

It took a long time for her to reach her post. The roads still were clogged with fugitives, with beggars, with sick and dying peasants, and with deserters.

The army was disintegrating. Holy Russia was dying. A godless nation was stirring in the womb.

For months at the front, she lived underground, and tried to get used to the thunder of the guns.

"Our nerves were tense," she says. "Our emotions were razor sharp, constantly whetted by the knowledge that the end of Russia was coming fast, by the increasing danger, by the growing hunger, and by the anger engendered in us through the shortage of supplies. But we still sang, as always. It was good to sing.

"We sang with the guns, the terrible Big Berthas. We would

sing a verse, or half a verse, and wait for the guns to join in with their 'boom, boom, boom' — just as people halt in singing "Deep in the Heart of Texas" and clap their hands in rhythm.

"We sang even when we could not hear our own voices — because of the armadas of planes overhead and the roar of the artillery."

In a rest camp not far from the front she saw a regiment of Tartars arrive and go into action.

They were big, fierce, handsome men, slim of waist and wide of shoulder. Their heads were shaven in the manner of tonsured monks; and they were adorned with ferocious mustaches.

They were dressed in sheepskin jackets, dyed red with vegetable dyes — as brilliant a red as the Cossacks wore — and slashed to hold the Tartar knives. Their trousers were blue. Their boots, made of horse leather, were white; and were kept immaculate. Red, blue, and white — the colors of Holy Russia.

The handles of their knives were of metal, beautifully decorated, and polished until they shone like the keen blades; or they were of bone, carved in fantastic designs. They made a wicked show against the red of their jackets; a much more wicked display than the long crooked blades they carried at their sides.

On their heads they wore high white sheepskin hats, something like the shakos worn by American drum majors on parade.

They arrived in a long string of freight cars. The horses were unloaded at the siding. The men sprang into the saddles, and at once began to slash and cut every man, woman, and child around them. They killed lustily until one of their officers commanded them to stop.

"Little ones," he said mildly, "you are killing Russian brothers!"

These men had come down from the Caucasus mountains. They knew nothing of Russia. They had come to kill. So they killed. No one but an officer could have stopped them.

They were Mohammedans. They lived in their wilderness paradise as Abraham and the patriarchs had lived. They were nomads, herders of sheep and goats, huntsmen, soldiers, the most marvelous horsemen in the world.

They had no fears, no inhibitions, no regard for anyone or anything outside their tribal laws. They owed obedience only to their own chosen leaders who had come up out of the ranks. At the word of these leaders they became as gentle as lambs.

There was a great scandal over their indiscriminate slaughter of Russian people. But nothing was done about it. No one was punished. Too many other atrocities were being perpetrated throughout Russia. The authorities were weak and confused. And the Tartars were desperately needed at the front.

Russia used the Tartars only in emergencies. When a flank was weakening or falling back or was in danger of annihilation, the Tartars were loosed and sent rushing into battle. And God help those in their paths.

Nurse de Hueck watched them ride into a nest of machine guns.

"The Germans," she says, "were on the near edge of a steep ridge, about five hundred yards across a plain, and they had been having their own sweet way all forenoon.

"If we had had airplanes we could have disposed of them with no trouble. But, needless to say, we had no planes.

"The Tartars ambled out of a clump of trees, each man

clinging to the belly of his horse so that he was invisible to the enemy. They went at a canter for a few hundred yards, not trying to keep any certain formation, yet keeping together as a formidable unit.

"The Germans apparently saw only the horses. They held their fire. I imagine they thought the herd had escaped and was running away. They expected to capture the animals and use them. Horses were as valuable to the Germans then as they were to us.

"Slowly, painfully slowly, the horses crossed the plain, leaping trenches where hundreds of dead and wounded Russians lay, jumping across shell holes and broken or abandoned guns.

"My body ached with suspense. I expected that at any moment the machine guns would spit forth murderous fire. Surely even the most ignorant Germans must realize that horses running away do not go so straightly to a mark.

"Presently the horses changed their pace to a gallop. A furious gallop. But still the Germans held their fire.

"Suddenly, at a shrill command, the hidden Tartars came out of concealment. They swung themselves into their saddles. Their long sabers were in their hands, flashing high. They were waving like so many little lightnings. And the men were screaming their savage war cries.

"Because of their sheepskin hats, every man of them looked at least seven feet tall above the saddle.

"Too late did the Germans see those hats, those red coats bristling with knives. Too late did they catch the glitter of sabers, hear the battle cries. The Tartars were among them, ruthless, exultant, cutting off arms, lopping off heads, riding on.

"The troops in support of the machine gunners fled as

from incarnate devils. The whole wing of the German army caught the contagion of panic. And our infantry, what was left of it, went running across the plain with bayonets.

"The Tartars halted, drunk with blood but not yet sated. They stayed to rest their horses, and to chop into little bits the bodies their knives had already slashed."

Nurse de Hueck, her knees too weak to hold her upright, sat down beneath a tree.

"Scratch a Russian and you'll find a Tartar," she reflected.

That saying might be true, but she did not believe it. Russia was to her, then, a land of mystics, a nation of saints. The murderous blood of the Tartars might be in the people; but they were in control of that blood.

A few days later she found the answer in herself.

She entered the nurses' quarters to find a drunken soldier struggling with a girl of fifteen, a peasant beauty who had been assigned as maid of all work to the nurses.

"The blood of my Tartar ancestors took command of me," she says. "It swept through me in an irresistible tide."

She sprang at the soldier and tore him from his prey. She whirled him around and struck him in the face. She threw him to the floor and jumped on him, sinking her boots into his middle. She picked him up and hit him again and again. She seemed to have the power of a dozen men, despite her tubercular lungs.

When her anger began to subside she picked up the soldier, as though he had no weight at all, and heaved him through the door.

"You filthy swine," she shouted, "I'll have you shot."

Attacking a woman was an offense punishable by death at that time and in that place.

The soldier rose and limped away. Nurse de Hueck turned

to the girl, wanting to comfort her. But the child backed
away. She was more terrified at the nurse's anger than she
had been at the soldier's lust.

Catherine flushed with shame. She, who had felt proud
to have such an iron control of her anger, had actually
wanted to kill. And if she had had a knife, she would have
used it as the Tartars did.

"We are all like that, we Russians," she says. "We are a
good people, a pious people. But, when we have been pushed
around too much, and when our passion for justice has been
at last aroused, we give way to the Tartar appetite for
blood — and we drench the world with it."

Ten minutes later the soldier came back and threw himself
at the nurse's feet. His face was bloody, and he had lost
two of his front teeth.

"In the name of God," he begged, "don't have me shot.
I was drunk. I wasn't myself. Is there no mercy in you,
Nurse de Hueck? I have an aged mother. And my little sisters
are dependent on me. If I am to be shot, they will surely
starve."

Catherine felt anger stirring in her again.

"Get out," she said.

The man placed his hands together as though praying
before an ikon.

"Mercy!"

"Get out," the nurse repeated. "I give you your life this
time. But — if ever again . . ."

He grabbed the hem of her skirt, kissed it with his repulsive
mouth, leaving bloodstains on it, and hurried away.

The two met again not many months later.

Imperial Russia was dead. Red Russia had just been born.
And the soldier had become the head of the local Commune,

with power of life or death over those dragged into his
presence.

The nurse slipped her father's revolver into her right sleeve,
when two soldiers came to fetch her to the Communist
headquarters which was not far from the hospital. She held
her arm in such a way that the weapon could slip into her
hand at need.

If she were to die she would die fighting, with her back
against a wall and her father's farewell present in her hand.

She was led into a dirty little room. The soldier was
sprawled in a chair, his boots on the top of a desk. Sur-
prisingly, he scrambled up and stood facing her. She thought
it was simply custom, that made him rise when she entered;
an old soldier's habit of showing respect for authority.

But when he bowed low, she realized that he respected
her, not any authority she might represent.

"I sent for you, Nurse," he said, "to remind you of a certain
incident."

He talked with a lisp, because of the absence of two front
teeth.

"I remember it," the nurse answered, as calmly as she
could.

"You did me a service," the soldier said. "You not only
spared my life when you might have taken it, but you kept
me from a crime. I have a sister the age of that little girl.
I should never have forgiven myself if I, drunken beast that
I was, had really harmed her.

"I admire you, Nurse de Hueck. You need not be afraid
of me. From this moment you are under my protection."

In her astonishment and relief the nurse relaxed the stiff-
ness of her right arm, and the pearl-handled gun dropped
upon the floor.

The soldier smiled as she picked it up.

"You may go," he said.

Before the week had passed one of the two soldiers, who had taken her to the Communist leader, came to the hospital. He came furtively making sure the nurse was alone before he talked to her. He spoke in whispers.

"We have found out," he said, "who it is that signed all those Red Cross passes for officers."

"Have you?"

"The passes were made out in the names of private soldiers and given to the officers. By these passes the bloodsuckers were enabled to pass through the Red lines, to lose themselves far from the front, and even to make their way out of the country."

"Indeed?"

"Indeed, Nurse de Hueck. And the nurse who wrote those passes is in great danger. Saunter out to the woods. You will find a horse there. Get on it and ride. Ride hard. Take the north road. Keep on it until you reach a farmhouse with a burned roof, near a point where three roads cross. There will be a dog outside the house, and a woman sitting on a bench. The woman will give you peasant clothes."

"Thank you," the nurse said.

She was already sauntering toward the woods.

❧ 9 ❧

PETROGRAD, when she returned to it, was a hostile, fearful city, filled with beggars, drunken soldiers, thieving children, and frightened people. Most of the shops were empty and boarded up. Many had been looted and burned. The street-cars were not running. And there was little food.

Aunt Vera was living alone in a mansion that had been stripped of everything valuable. Catherine's home, to which she had come as a bride, was cold and empty. Her mother and her brothers were living at Antrea. Her father was somewhere in Petrograd, Aunt Vera told her, disguised as a workingman, living how he could. And Serge was in one of the schools which had not yet been closed.

"I have some things at Tsarkoe-Selo," Aunt Vera said. "I need them, and I am going to get them. Will you come with me, or must I go alone?"

"I will go with you, of course, if we can pass the Red guards."

Tsarkoe-Selo, where the imperial family had been imprisoned, was a suburb of Petrograd. One could go there in twenty minutes or so on the railroad.

The two women set out early. They arrived at the depot without encountering any danger. But there the Red guards barred their entry, bayonets in their hands, grim smiles on their faces. They demanded to see the necessary passes.

Aunt Vera was as unfitted for the revolution as the veriest child. She was consistently ignorant of all that it implied. She had changed outwardly in many ways. Hunger had enfeebled her. Cold and terror and grief had aged her. Yet, inwardly, she had not changed in the slightest. She saw no reason why a lady shouldn't go where she pleased, do what she wished to do, whether there was a revolution or not.

The soldiers didn't frighten her. They made her angry.

She drew herself up to her full height, and in her most aristocratic and overbearing tones demanded to know why such ugly and desperate ruffians dared to stop her, or even to speak to her.

"I will have you know," she said, "that I come from Smolny!"

She could not more clearly have confessed her state in life. She could not have told the guards more plainly that she was one of the enemies they sought. Smolny was the school she attended in her youth. It was the most snobbish school in Russia. Only the most select of the daughters of the most select of the noble families were permitted to enter its sacrosanct portals.

The young baroness fully expected to hear again the shout of the guards — "Ho, another bloodsucking aristocrat" — to hear a volley of shots, or to see somebody draw a sword and cut off her auntie's imperious head.

Only a few days before she had heard that cry and the shots had followed. She had been hurrying along the street, and a gang of drunken men had stopped her. She was wearing a fur coat; so she must be an enemy. They fired at her. She threw up a hand to shield her face. A bullet went through her palm. She fainted. The blood streamed

across her face. The men evidently thought she was dead.
They went off and left her.

Her bandaged hand throbbed madly now, as she waited
for the depot guards to fire. She didn't blame Aunt Vera
for her betraying pride and anger. She might have expected
just such a remark.

But the reaction of the guards was fantastic, ridiculous.

They froze to rigid attention. Then they saluted the two
ladies as they would have saluted Lenin himself. They bel-
lowed orders down the line which froze other soldiers, and
got the baronesses willing and elaborate courtesies.

Aunt Vera was not astonished. Nor did she feel at all
triumphant. So far as she was concerned nothing unusual
had happened. This was the treatment she had always been
accorded when people realized who she was.

She did not know, and her niece never told her, that the
noble little ladies had been cleared out of Smolny, and that
the school had become the headquarters of Nicolai Lenin.
She did not know, and would not have believed, that the
reverence and awe given by her voice to the memory of
her old school clicked, in the minds of the guards, with
the reverence and awe they felt for the name of Lenin.

So far as they were concerned the two women were not
of the old aristocracy but of the new. They were friends
of Lenin and nothing was too good for them.

They arrived safely at Tsarkoe-Selo. They found Aunt
Vera's home untouched. They gathered up a few fur pieces
and a few jars of preserves, and carried them back to
Petrograd.

Even to the last, Catherine declares, Aunt Vera kept her
integrity. She ate dogs and cats and mice, as her friends
and relatives did. She feasted with them on the potato peel-

ings Catherine managed to retrieve from garbage cans at night. But her spirit fattened on other things, even when her body starved.

Early one cold morning Catherine sneaked out of the house and went to a little Polish church. There were but half a dozen other worshipers there: bundled, blurry figures with frosty breaths. The church was lighted by the two candles on the altar and the red votive lamp that told of the presence of the Blessed Sacrament.

The priest, a frail old man, came to the altar unaccompanied by an acolyte. And the Mass was begun.

At the Consecration, as the priest lifted the Host, a squad of Red soldiers came marching down the center aisle, their boots waking a million echoes.

"Stop that nonsense," the leader yelled.

The priest held the Wafer steadily.

There was a shot.

The Host fell from the priest's fingers. It dropped to the altar steps, on edge, and rolled like a tiny wheel down the red-carpeted stairs to the lowest step. It lay there, a gleaming round white spot on the crimson nap.

And on the shining white chasuble of the priest a round red spot grew and spread. The priest slowly lowered his hands. His body tottered and fell.

Two soldiers vaulted over the altar rail. One kicked the body, and twisted his heavy heel on the bread made Flesh. The other stood guard, an automatic rifle menacing those in the pews.

The leader turned to the worshipers, laughing satanically.

"There is no God," he shouted. "I've killed Him."

The church echoed and re-echoed with the laughter and shouts of his men.

Then an old man in the first pew, a very old man, raised his voice in a shrill quavering prayer.

"Father, forgive them, even if they know what they do!"

The soldiers left the altar and joined their comrades. The leader shouted a command, and the Red guards marched out of the church.

The old man left the pew, opened the gates in the altar railing, genuflected, threw himself on his knees, and wept. Catherine and the others gathered about him.

He took up the Host, broke such parts of It as were not already broken or ground into the carpet, and gave the Particles to those around him.

They made such reparation as they could, with prayer, with washing and scrubbing of the carpet, and with tears. One of the women wet her kerchief in the blood of the martyred priest; and Catherine said a silent prayer:

"Soldier priest of Christ, pray for Russia. Pray for us."

It was still dark outside. There was still time to forage for food. Catherine found a few cabbage leaves; but they were frozen to the side of the can and she could not release them. Her right hand was still bandaged. The fingers of her left hand were numb — and they still shook with the anger that had gripped her at the murder and the sacrilege she had witnessed. The anger, and the fear.

She left the cabbage leaves where they were and hurried to Aunt Vera's.

They sat there in silence, two women in a once luxurious apartment, three floors above the street level. There was a grand piano in the corner. It had been made by an artist. It was fashioned of costly woods. It was worth thousands of rubles. But the soldiers had not wanted it. It had no value at all now. It might do to keep a fire burning in the grate —

when one had the strength to hack it into kindling. There were two rickety chairs in which the women sat. They would be used for kindling too, sometime soon. There were ikons on the wall, but no vigil lights before them. There was a fireplace, but it held only ashes.

A long time they sat in silence, two thin, ill-clad, hungry, frightened, wondering women; one very old, one very young.

They heard a footstep on the stairs.

It was soft, stealthy, slow. It was coming up.

The women turned their heads toward the door, listening intently. Their breathing changed. They avoided each other's eyes. Their bodies stiffened.

That was the way it started. A footstep on the stairway. An informer, a spy, a secret agent of the police. Later, other footsteps would come, heavy and quick and brutal to the ear. And tomorrow, or the day after, some relative would read their names in the lists in the Soviet newspaper. The list of the proscribed and the dead.

The footsteps halted on the first landing, and the younger woman dared to breathe again. She looked at the nearest ikon. Her lips moved but made no sound. Her bandaged hand was lifted as though in warning.

The footsteps were coming up another flight.

Catherine's arm instinctively moved to her boot top. But the revolver was not there. She had forgotten that long ago, she had exchanged it for half a frozen turnip.

What had she not traded for food! The family silver had bought a few dried herrings and a head of lettuce. Paintings, gems, lamps, furs, rugs, expensive bits of furniture had bought potatoes, cabbages, a handful of beans, a pound of cheap green tea.

Again the footsteps halted; but this time neither of the women relaxed nor stirred.

A brief halt. Then, distinct, implacable, but slow and soft, the footsteps came up the last flight. They paused outside the door.

Someone was breathing heavily out there on the landing, resting limbs tired with the long climb, getting ready for what?

The woman saw the doorknob turn. It turned silently, slowly. The door opened. Slowly. Silently.

A woman stood inside the room. A woman heavily bundled. Her drab clothes were covered with snow. Her kerchief seemed made of snow.

Without a word she swung the door shut behind her.

Masha!

That it should be Masha, of all the people in the world!

Masha had been one of the maids at the Kolyschkine apartment. Catherine's mother had nursed her when the baby came, had arranged her marriage to the baby's father; and Catherine had been proud when Masha asked her to be the baby's godmother.

So Masha had joined the Communists. She had ferreted out her friends. The police would come soon. Or the soldiers. There would be no escape.

Slowly, stealthily, softly, Masha walked to the piano. She did not look at the young woman, nor at the old one. She said no word. She took from beneath her cloak a bundle wrapped in a wet newspaper, showering snow on the bare floor as she did so. She put the package on the piano. She turned and left the room, as menacing as when she came.

The women listened to her footsteps going down the

stairs. And for a long time after they ceased to be heard, they sat unmoving in their chairs.

Then the younger went to the piano and examined the package. It could not be a bomb. It did not tick. It might be anti-Communist literature, planted for the Reds to find. But it did not seem to be anything of the sort.

Suddenly she began to tear at the wet newspapers, the pain in her bandaged hand forgotten.

Masha had brought a ham. A whole baked ham!

❧ 10 ❧

A MONTH or two after the Communists had routed the Kerensky forces and assumed the supreme power in Russia, the baron, Boris de Hueck, managed to reach Petrograd. He had been gassed, and was very weak. But he felt strong enough to flee to his estate in Finland, at Kiskiile-Kula, near Bejke, not more than a hundred miles away from the Kolyschkine estate at Antrea.

Catherine's father, in one of his infrequent appearances at the De Hueck flat, had said that Antrea was in "White territory," and everybody there was safe. Kiskiile-Kula, therefore, they reasoned, must also be a safe refuge from the Communists.

The baron and his young wife asked Aunt Vera to accompany them. But she refused. She was too old for that long walk, she said. She might have added that she was too weak, and that she preferred to die in the land she had known and loved rather than live in a land she did not know and could never love.

They left her, with tears, to die alone of starvation and exposure in the cold and empty flat.

Their first destination was a farm at Bielo-Ostrov, on the Finnish border. The baron had some friends there who had volunteered to get him and his wife across the line and put them on a train that would take them to their estate.

They traveled mostly at night, dressed as peasants. It was cold; and despite their heavy clothes they suffered. The snows were deep, and they could not go fast. They had no food, and they found few places where they could sleep during the day — but they heartened themselves with thoughts of a long rest at Bielo-Ostrov and plenty of food.

They were in constant terror, especially when they saw people coming toward them.

"Only one incident of that trip remains in my memory," Catherine says. "That was the finish of it."

They came out of the woods to see the lights of a house shining hospitably a few hundred yards away. They stood in the snow a long time, like hungry and frightened wolves — thinking of fat fowls turning on a spit and of heaps of warm fresh cakes and of warm, soft beds; yet fearing to go a step forward lest there be Red soldiers about the place.

The frosted stars and the half of a moon lighted the snows between them and their refuge. They would have to cross it. If they were seen they might be fired at, but they had to take the chance.

They waded through the drifts as cautiously as they could, falling every time they heard a noise, rising up, going slowly ahead. When they were only a few feet away from the back door of the farmhouse they lay still a long time, listening. There were people in the kitchen; but it was impossible to tell whether they were friends or foes.

"We could smell borsch cooking," Catherine remembers. "It maddened us to recklessness. We went to the door and knocked. Softly."

Ivan Ivanovitch, the baron's friend, opened the door but a trifle. He recognized Boris and put his finger to his lips.

"There are soldiers here," he said. "Hide in the pigsty. Quickly. I will come as soon as I can."

It was an ordinary pigsty, but it had a board roof over

it. It was as foul and repulsive a place as could be imagined;
and Catherine had an impulse to sit down in the mire and
straw and weep. Instead she laughed.

"We wanted food," she said. "It is all around us. We wanted
a bed. We've found it."

For hours they stood up, the pigs crowding about them,
and held their noses with their mittened hands. Ivan must
come out of the house at any minute.

The moon slipped behind a cloud. The stars were blurred.
Snow began to fall; and in a little time it was raining and
sleeting, and the wind was blowing through the pigsty
like a gale.

The two aristocrats slipped down into the mire through
sheer fatigue and slept.

For three days and three nights they stayed in that pigsty.
Their clothes, their hands, their faces, were covered with
filth and vermin. They could scarcely stand the odor of the
pigs — or of each other. But they dared not leave.

Twice the Red soldiers came near, and on both occasions
the baron and baroness burrowed into the muck as far as
they could, and covered themselves with rubbish.

"When I discovered that I was covered with crawling
vermin as well as with the dirt of the pigs and of the sty,"
Catherine says, "I thought of my childhood, the maids who
used to draw me a warm bath, rub me dry with a big
coarse towel, powder me with fragrant powder, comb out
my locks and brush them, and caress my ears with choice
perfume. I thought of them, and wondered if I had always
treated them as equals, or even as friends. I wondered if
I were not being justly punished for my sins against charity —
and whether or not the good Lord was teaching me a lesson
in values."

Only once did Ivan come out to feed his fugitive friends. It was early evening, and he was carrying two steaming bowls of borsch. But, as he approached the pigsty, a Red soldier fell into step with him.

"Is it thus, Comrade Ivan Ivanovitch, you feed your swine?" he asked.

Ivan managed to smile and to shrug his shoulders. The fugitives, hiding behind a fat sow — and holding onto her legs so she would not rush toward the food — could see him plainly.

"Pigs are only pigs," he replied, "and deserve no better than slop. But a clumsy servant broke the salt shaker. The salt poured into the soup. So, Comrade, it is fit only for hogs."

He poured it carelessly into the trough, and the two went back to the house.

"I watched the pigs licking up our dinner," Catherine says, "but I wasn't hungry. When you feel terror, you can't feel hunger."

A few hours before daybreak on the last night, Ivan came hurrying out to the sty.

"Go now," he said. "Down the gully and across the river. Then you will be in Finland, and safe. But go at once."

There was no moon and the stars were not shining. In the darkness the fugitives might have fallen over the edge of the gully and broken an arm or a leg. But there was a heavy brush, and by holding onto bushes they negotiated the descent in safety. The last few feet of the incline were covered with hard snow and ice. They "just slid down."

Finnish sentries across the river heard the noise they made, and fired a number of shots.

Catherine had expected the river would be frozen. But it was a mountain torrent hurrying toward the sea with too much velocity to let ice form. It was no more than ankle deep, and it was only twenty feet wide.

They crossed it on their hands and knees, pausing every little while to let the icy water wash the dirt and the ordure and the stench from their clothing and their skins.

They arrived in Finland soaked to their insides and festooned with icicles; and said a prayer of thanks.

Finland was a part of Russia, but it had its own self-government, its own customs, its own little army. And there was talk of a war for independence. There were Red armies in the territory, but most of the Finns were anti-Communist, indeed anti-Russian; and it was said that some of them were trying to arrange an alliance with Germany against the Soviets.

Catherine led the way to the railroad station — through the window of which she had observed a great round stove with a cherry-red belly.

Finnish soldiers stopped her and the baron.

"Halt. Who are you? What are you doing here?"

Catherine answered in Finnish and made good friends.

"So it was you then, little one, we heard sliding down the gully a little while ago — you and your father?"

"Yes," Catherine answered. "We were running from Russian soldiers."

Before long she and Boris were dressed in warm dry clothes, sitting near the glowing stove, and eating thick sandwiches with reindeer meat between the pieces of soft, black bread.

When the train pulled out, they were aboard.

It was early in the afternoon of the next day that they caught sight of the house and the buildings on their estate.

"Safe at last," Catherine said. "It seems too good to be true."

She saw cows wending their way toward the barn, a boy with a stick bringing up the rear of the procession. She saw flocks of chickens and geese.

And she saw men and women rushing toward them.

"They recognize you," she said to the baron. "They are hurrying to welcome us home!"

The baron recognized some of them as they came near. Old friends. Old neighbors.

But the women wore red ribbons on their clothes. The men had red rags tied about their sleeves.

They were friends and servants no longer. They were Communists. They were enemies, masters. And they welcomed the baron and baroness only as prisoners.

"There was something that resembled a trial," Catherine says. "We were found guilty of being enemies of the people, and were condemned to be shot. The judge, the leader of the local Commune, however, commuted that sentence — or rather changed it. We were to die of starvation. That would be more fun, he thought, and it might give him some material profit, which would be denied him if we were summarily shot. He thought the baron had hidden jewels and silverware on the estate, and that, when he was sufficiently starved, he would divulge the hiding place."

The two who had fled so far and endured so much in an effort to find freedom were locked in a room in their own house. Water was brought to them every day, in order that it might sustain but not nourish them, and they might not die too soon. And every day the judge, who had always been a ne'er-do-well, came into the room to spit on the baron, to curse him, and to threaten him with torture if he did not reveal the cache of his treasures.

"There is no pain in starving," Catherine says. "Not for the first few days. Your head becomes clear. You think logically. You crave food, of course, but you feel you can live without it if you have to. You remember that Christ fasted for forty days in the desert, and you determine to imitate Him.

"A few days later your head becomes light, and your body swells in places. Your arms, for instance. You can stick a finger into your flesh and make a dent that stays there for an hour or so. Then you begin to feel pain, like a knife inside and across your middle. At first, you feel this pain once a day. Then two or three times a day. Afterward you feel it every hour or so. The body, having nothing to digest, is digesting itself.

"Your hair falls out in batches. Your teeth loosen. And you can't help it, sometimes, if you go crazy and gnaw at the wood in the room.

"One morning a little dog scampered in through the door, when a man came with the water. He was carrying a bone in his mouth.

"Can you imagine a husband and wife, too weak to do anything but lie in their beds most of the time, suddenly getting strength enough to spring up, wrest the bone away from the animal, and fight each other desperately for it?

"And can you imagine how they felt at finding not a particle of meat or gristle on the bone?

"If you can, you will not wonder that I was several times tempted to use the mercy of the chimney gases to end my suffering. It would be so easy, I thought, to die that way."

The meditation that had begun in the agony of the pigsty was continued in this prison. Catherine, for the first time in her seventeen or eighteen years, began to blame herself and her people for all that had happened in the Communist revolution.

Her people had always been powerful and rich. They had given of their substance to the poor, of course, but out of a sense of charity, or *noblesse oblige,* never through a sense of justice.

Through their arrogance and pride and greed for lands and goods and slaves, they had ground the faces of the poor into the dust. They had denied the peasants the rights they had fought to win for themselves. They had regarded their kindred in Christ almost as cattle.

Now it was these people who held the whip, the rich and haughty who suffered. All the rights and privileges and all the wealth amassed by the mighty during the centuries, and all the power they had so mercilessly exercised, were gone.

And this, it seemed to her, was justice.

Terrible crimes had attended this sudden overturn of fortunes; and famine and pestilence and anarchy and atheism had followed it. But that made the punishment of the wicked rich no less just.

"I could not know then," she says, "that the poor would be even poorer because of this revolution. I could not know that millions would starve to death, that millions would be imprisoned, and that millions of others would be made slaves. I knew only that the poor and impotent had risen, had toppled the rich and mighty from their seats; and I thought that, after a few years of bloodshed and lawlessness, justice might prevail and Russia become once more holy. I was so elated at the thought that I sung our Lady's *Magnificat* aloud.

"'He hath wrought mightily with His arm; He hath scattered the proud in the conceit of their hearts.

"'He hath put down the mighty from their seats, and hath exalted the humble.

" 'He hath filled the hungry with good things, and the rich He hath sent away empty.' "

Now Catherine has another idea of Russia.

"The country was possessed of a devil," she says. "The devil was chased away. The country was swept clean of him. The devil, seeing it clean, returned, and brought seven other devils with him. They all took up their abode there — and they hope to extend their kingdom throughout the world."

Until the revolution, Catherine reflected, she had been a mere Lady Bountiful, giving herself pleasure by distributing money, clothes, food, and medicines to the poor, out of her abundance; and taking pleasure in nursing poor and grateful villagers when she could spare the time. She had never known what it was to be poor, to be hungry, to wear rags, to be helpless in every way. She had not loved the poor as she loved herself, nor had she ever felt herself one of the poor, their sister.

"I was just as responsible for the revolution and all the woes it engendered," Catherine was convinced, "as any others of my class. I had heard the people crying for bread, and I had scarcely listened.

"I had heard them crying for other things, for lands of their own, for decent prices for their crops, for decent schools for their children, for equal opportunities with their richer brothers, for equal rights before the law; and I had not listened, I had not answered.

"I had not realized that the voice of the people was indeed the voice of God.

"Yes, I was responsible. If the poor were ignorant, brutal, and merciless in their new power, I had helped to make them so. I had failed in my duties as a Christian. Let me now do the only thing left for me to do, ask God for the grace to forgive those who trespassed against me, even as He forgave me; and offer up my sufferings in part atonement for my sins and the sins of my people.

"It seemed strange that I should learn the first principles of Christianity in these hours of my life. I was doomed to die. I had learned the truth too late. But I gave thanks I could still bend my head to His holy will, and die the death He meant for me."

Once she had resigned herself to die, not by gas but through lack of food, her fate took another turn. A detachment of the White army marched in, scattered the Reds, and rescued her and the baron.

"They came into the house, bringing us food and wine," she says, "and we did not believe it. We were afraid to touch what they gave us.

"Later they brought in the man who had judged and condemned us and who had so thoroughly abused the baron."

A young officer saluted the baron and asked what should be done with the prisoner.

"What has he done?" the baron asked.

Apparently he, too, had done some meditating.

The officer looked surprised. "Isn't this the man who ordered you to be starved?"

"I never saw him before," the baron lied. "But I don't think much of him. Shoot him, if you like. But why waste a bullet on a ruffian like that?"

❧ 11 ❧

SOMETIME in the late spring of 1918, Catherine and her husband made their way to the house at Antrea. Catherine weighed about ninety pounds. Her hair was still falling out. Her teeth were loose. Her face was pale and wrinkled like an old woman's.

The White army medical nurses had cared for her and Boris for several weeks but had not been able to feed them properly.

Catherine's mother came to the door; and her daughter could only stand and weep. She did not trust herself to speak.

"What can I do for you, Lady?" the elder woman asked. "You look hungry. I could give you something to eat. And you are cold, and your husband too. Have you traveled far? Come in."

"Mother!" Catherine found her tongue. "Don't you know me at all?"

For a long time her mother stared at her. "Katia! Is it really you?"

Her father came to the door, an old man with a shawl around his massive shoulders. He was dying even then. He had carried Serge through the snows that covered the Gulf of Finland, in his flight from Petrograd, and had been fighting pneumonia ever since.

That night the family sang a fervent *Te Deum Laudamus*. The defection of Russia had permitted the Germans to take many divisions of heavily armed troops from the eastern to the western front; and the Allies felt this might be the beginning of a German victory.

For four years the Allies had fought. They had lost millions of men. They had exhausted billions of dollars' worth of ammunition and supplies. They were weak and impoverished, and it seemed hopeless for them to fight on. True, the United States had come into the war, and was preparing a mighty army. But none of those war-weary British, French, Italians, and Portuguese expected to see the American army in actual conflict. They did not know much about Americans. They didn't know the spirit of the people, had no idea of their resourcefulness, their energy, nor of the speed with which they did the impossible.

They believed they were fighting a lost cause; but they intended to fight as long as they could.

It seemed evident to them that the Germans, after the treaty of Brest-Litovsk, would be able to march through Russia into Finland and thus capture the ice-free ports in the far north, and take the enormous depots of provisions and war materials the Allies had dumped for the feeding and equipping of the armies of the Czar. From the ports they would be enabled to set their U-boats loose for havoc. They might even break the British blockade.

Even if they failed in this the food supplies in Archangel and Murmansk would nullify the effects of the blockade to a great extent. It would feed Germany and Austria for months and furnish them valuable new equipment.

"We are likely to discover," a British general said, "that in trying to strengthen Russia we have given added might to Germany — and furnished our enemies with a way to attack the American transports. If German submarines slip out of

Archangel or Murmansk, they might encircle our mine fields, evade the British fleet, and speed directly toward the Yankee troops sailing to our aid. We must protect Archangel and Murmansk, therefore, at all costs."

At all costs! A force must be sent to Finland; but it would have to be a limited force, for only a few men could be spared from the battle front.

There was a faint hope that the expedition might achieve success, if it could be augmented by White Russian or Finnish troops, and by other volunteers with anti-German sympathies.

A call for volunteers was broadcast throughout Finland and the neutral Scandinavian countries.

At Antrea, Baron and Baroness de Hueck heard the call, and determined to answer it.

For the last time Catherine knelt for her father's blessing.

"Go with God," he said simply. He seemed to realize this was the last time on earth he would ever see his daughter.

At Helsinki, Catherine enrolled in the expeditionary force as an interpreter and a nurse; and Boris joined as an officer of engineers.

In undergoing a physical examination Catherine learned, to her great astonishment, that the tuberculosis had disappeared. What had cured her? The cold of Finland? The good food and the long rest at her father's house? Or those weeks of starvation? She does not know.

Through the help of British agents the De Huecks got to Narvick, Norway. From there they were taken on a fishing trawler to Murmansk and attached to the forces of the White Russian general, Miller.

Catherine was made an official interpreter at general headquarters, and was also assigned as a nurse in the British hospital, miles away from headquarters. She used a handcar to

Catherine in Her Chautauqua Days

George de Hueck
with His Mother

George in Canadian Uniform
in World War II

travel up and down the narrow-gauge railroad between the two points. A military train sometimes was used; but the hand-car was more easily available.

"It was a war-made community," Catherine said, describing Murmansk. "All the houses were of wood, and some of them, especially the nurses' home, were scant protection from the severe cold. It was a most interesting region, in that all the trees and plants were of the dwarf variety, and that the sun never set for months. It would go down to the far rim of the ocean, and then begin to rise."

There was no fighting when Catherine arrived; but there were enemies in the making. They were not Germans, but various detachments of the Soviet armies. At first they showed only covert hostility, but later there were gory battles.

"My dual job," she says, "kept me busy all day and most of the night. At headquarters, sometimes, I had to use all the diplomacy I had learned from my father."

A British general would say to her, "Tell that so and so Frog and that stubborn Russian ass that the plan we are going to use is the one I suggested."

Catherine would turn to the French general and the Russian general in turn.

"His excellency, the British general, wishes your excellency to know that his opinion is unchanged, much as he would like to defer to your excellency's idea."

"Make the English pig understand we are proceeding according to my plan," the Frenchman would answer. "And tell the species of camel I like neither his attitude nor his beefy red face."

And the Russian would bellow. "Tell that old maid with the mustaches and the military pants that there is but one way to proceed — my way."

The Russians and Finns in the camp regarded the Tommies as something less than men. It was disgusting, they said, to see men who lived on such things as tea and biscuits with jam or marmalade, and cans of bully beef or salmon. A real man needed black bread and lots of it, and great bowls of soup with cabbage in it and big chunks of meat; and tea that was tea, not dishwater.

Above all, they despised the British soldier's inability to drink like a he-man should.

Four sentries broke into a storehouse of rum they were guarding one cold night. Two Russians. Two Englishmen. They finished two small kegs of rum.

The Englishmen died the next day.

The Russians felt no ill effects, not even a headache.

Once the Russians complained bitterly about the Scotties.

"If they are men," they said to the British commander, "make them put away their skirts. If they are women, make them shave off their mustaches."

Their contempt for the Tommies vanished after the first battle.

Catherine describes that engagement as "short and bloody." She watched it from a ridge top, not far from the place where the English force was drawn up and waiting.

"The English," she says, "were on top of a gentle slope leading down to a long wide field. The Russians were below, and in considerable force compared to the few English soldiers they were attacking.

"The Reds were big men, fiercely whiskered, picturesquely dressed. The English were mostly undersized. Each man shaved every morning. And there was nothing at all picturesque about them — except their kilts.

"The Russians were a few thousand feet away when I first

saw them. At the command of their leaders they began to charge up the slope, running, shouting frightful oaths.

"I happened to be looking at the British subaltern when he made up his mind. He looked like a boy just out of prep school. He stood in front of his men, and saluted them. They returned the salute. He turned, lifted his little swagger stick — his only weapon — and led them over the ridge and down the slope. They walked into battle, as they would walk to work.

"The boy lieutenant fell forward and died. The men went on without his guiding, calm, unhurried, deadly. They met the Russian charge unafraid, and smashed it; then went at their bloody job in earnest. When they were through there was no living Red upon the slope."

There were spies in Murmansk, and saboteurs. And Catherine, accidentally, brought a few of them to justice.

She was at the nurses' home. She was wanted at headquarters. She went to the railroad depot to get the handcar, but it was not there. She would have to wait for the military train, which was not due for an hour.

It was cold, so she crawled into the hay piled on one side of the station. She had scarcely done so when four men entered the depot. They were talking in Finnish. About dynamite! A great quantity of dynamite had been stolen from a warehouse several nights before. Catherine listened attentively.

When the train arrived she waited until the men had boarded it. Then she brushed the hay off her clothes, let herself out of the depot, and came running up — panting as though she had come a long way — and swung herself onto the caboose.

The men were still talking. She pretended not to understand the language when one of the four spoke to her. They continued their conversation.

When she stepped off the caboose she fell, deliberately, and took a long time to get up and arrange her woolen stockings. When the quartet was far enough away not to be suspicious of her, she followed them. She saw the building they entered, waited a while; and, when they did not emerge, hurried to headquarters and told her story.

The men were arrested, tried, found guilty, and punished. The dynamite was recovered.

In the fall of 1919, the Communists had broken the threat of Kolchak and Wrangle, and all the other White leaders, and were on their way to Murmansk.

The need for the expeditionary force in that region had vanished with the total defeat of Germany. There was nothing to do but pack what supplies there were, destroy what could not be moved, and evacuate all personnel.

Boris was suffering from pleurisy. He was put aboard the hospital ship. His wife was assigned to that ship as a nurse. The destination was Scotland.

Catherine stood at the rail as the ship pulled away from the wooden city, wondering if she would ever see her native land again, wondering what God had in store for her in Scotland or in England or wherever else in the world He might deign to send her.

There were two friends aboard. One was a patient, an American boy who had enlisted in a British regiment, and who had "wangled" his way to Finland with the expedition.

She had seen him first in the hospital. He was delirious with fever; and he kept saying, "Shake a leg, Nurse, shake a leg." Occasionally he added, "And make it snappy."

Nurse de Hueck spoke English well; but this didn't seem to make much sense. Shake a leg and make it snappy. What could it possibly mean?

For a long time she listened to the boy, then went to the bed, uncovered one of his legs, and shook it. The patient immediately went to sleep.

The nurse made a record of the incident, and discussed it the following day with her superior.

"And for the rest of my days in Murmansk," she reports, "everybody laughed when they saw me and said 'Shake a leg, Nurse, and make it snappy.'"

The other friend was a girl of twenty, Dunia Bikova, a native of Murmansk. She had been employed in the nurses' quarters; and when the port had been evacuated, she asked Catherine to "take her along."

"What can I do?" Catherine asked. "I can't take you, Dunia."

"Then maybe you have friends who will take me," Dunia said. "I cannot stay here. The Communists are coming. They will make me a Communist. And I would rather die. They will make me a Communist, or they will kill me. Get somebody to take me to England, or I will kill myself."

Catherine spoke of her to an English officer.

"Can she cook?" he asked.

"She can cook," Catherine said. "And she can wash clothes, scrub, run errands, and do anything else around the house."

"I say," the officer said. "Just the thing. There's a shortage of maids and cooks in London, I understand. Tell her to come aboard."

Boris was still sick when the ship docked in Scotland. He was taken to the Craleigh Hospital in Edinburgh, and Catherine was assigned there as a nurse to the Serbian patients brought from Murmansk.

Boris was still weak when he was discharged from the hospital; but neither he nor Catherine felt there was any cause for complaint in that. There were so many others who needed the bed he occupied and the nurses who attended him — men much more unfortunate than he.

"We have so much to be thankful for," Catherine said to him. "We are alive. We are safe. We have our tickets to London — and all these Russian rubles. They should bring us a lot of money; don't you think?"

She counted the rubles. There were ten thousand and more of them. The money they had brought from Antrea, and the money for their services in the White Russian army at Murmansk.

She could hardly wait until she got to the bank to change those rubles into pounds, shillings, and pence. But alas, she didn't know how far the ruble had fallen from its former rate. All the bank would give her for those ten thousand and more rubles was a little over three pounds sterling — about $15 in American money.

They arrived in London in a fog. They didn't know anybody there. They didn't know the city. They had no plans, no jobs, no definite way of making a living. They had no nationality, for, inasmuch as they were not Communists they could not be classed as Russians.

But they were happy.

⇛ 12 ⇚

ONE of the problems that bothered Catherine in the strange new world of Edinburgh was the obtaining of a wardrobe.

"I must have been an odd sight when I came off the ship," she says. "I must have been even an odder sight when I left my father's home at Antrea for the Murmansk expedition.

"There were no old clothes at that house. Mother had given them all away. I had to use my own devices to dress myself. I went into Helsinki wearing shoes I had fashioned out of heavy curtains. My dress had been a summer bathrobe. And everything else I had on me had been made from something else.

"At Helsinki an Australian soldier gave me his hat, his high boots, and a pair of officers' shoes. They were small, the boots and the shoes, but too large for me. In Murmansk I acquired a Russian nurse's uniform, and later a British nurse's outfit.

"I had the boots, the uniforms, and the old campaign hat when I landed in Scotland. The people laughed at me, naturally, but they were generous too. They gave me dresses, underwear, good shoes, and even a hat with flowers on it.

"Boris didn't have this problem at all. He took the insignia off his jacket, and he was in civvies."

The Y.M.C.A. in London provided the refugees with a room, in courteous acknowledgment of the fact that Catherine had helped its secretaries in Murmansk; and she found a job with the Russian Red Cross, sewing underwear for Wrangle's forces. For this she was given a daily lunch and a daily shilling.

She had brought some jewelry from Antrea. She pawned a few pieces, but only a few. She clung to those treasures as she clung to the food she had carried with her from Murmansk. When she had money to spend for food she bought not one or two doughnuts, but one or two dozen. What she didn't eat immediately she hid.

This was, of course, a reaction from the weeks of starvation. She used to wake, sometimes, in a dream that she was dying again of hunger, and she would get up and visit her various food caches.

"Dunia," she says, "helped us more than the jewels. She came to us wherever we happened to be and insisted on working for us. We paid her when we could, which was not often. Frequently — after she had left the family of the English officer — she took jobs by the day or the week, and gave her wages to us. And, when she had no money to bring us, she brought us food or clothes."

Through the Red Cross, Catherine was able to get news of some of her relatives and friends.

"The stories I heard," she recounts, "made me realize over and over how fortunate I was.

"The Princess X was singing in a low dive on the Bund in Shanghai. The beautiful young wife of Count Y, formerly an officer in a cavalry regiment, was selling herself in Constantinople. Her husband had been gassed and wounded. He was a hopeless invalid. His wife had not been trained, as I had been, to do a hundred different things. She had never worked at all. This was the only way she could support the man she loved. And I don't think God will be too harsh with her on judgment day.

"Baron X was dead, and his children scattered.

"Two aunts of mine were dead. They had pooled their assets after the revolution and found a room where they could live with their children. They had sold or traded everything they had, except one fur coat. They wore it in turn, when they went out onto the streets to sell the Communist newspapers.

"One put the coat over her naked body and walked the streets all day with her bundle of papers. The other stayed naked in the naked house with the babies huddled about her — all of them trying to sleep on the cold naked floor — until it was her turn to put on the coat and sell the papers through the night.

"My aunts had died of hunger and exposure. The children had been taken by the Soviets."

In her hours away from the Red Cross, Catherine looked for work, but could not find it. She was as strong as Dunia — who never failed to find a job — and she was as young and willing as the other girl. She was incomparably better educated, she could do things Dunia could not do, but employers turned her away.

London was filled with returned soldiers, men with one arm or one leg and rows of ribbons on their coats, selling matches.

"I felt ashamed to be seeking work for myself when these brave fellows couldn't get anything better to do than sell matches," she says. "I thought, many a time, that I was trying to take the bread out of their mouths, and the mouths of their wives and children. Perhaps that was why I always failed."

To better her chances she took an Oxford course in English, with special attention to the acquiring of a bigger vocabulary and the correct pronunciation of words. She spoke with a French accent, people told her.

"I fell asleep over these lessons one night," she says, "and dreamed that I was in church praying for a miracle. No, for two miracles. I woke to find the prayers were in my heart. I was praying for a job that would enable me to support myself and Boris, who was still too ill to work; and I was praying I might have at least one child."

"It's no use," Boris said, when he had heard about her dreams. "The doctors have said you cannot have a child. And you have learned there isn't a job in all London. We'll just have to go back to war. Wrangle is still fighting. Maybe, through the Russian embassy, we can join him."

"He's still fighting," Catherine said, "but how long will he last?"

Boris shrugged his shoulders.

They walked to the embassy that morning. The man in charge received them cordially, but gave them no encouragement.

"Sorry," he said. "We are not recruiting. We are expecting orders to close this shebang any day. Wrangle is at the end of his rope."

Catherine didn't quite understand. What was a shebang? And Wrangle at the end of his rope — had he hanged himself?

She noted the way the man looked at Boris. He realized that Boris was sick, she thought. That was why he said he wasn't recruiting. But he might consider recruiting a strong young nurse.

Then she noticed that it was at Boris' hand the man was staring, not at his face.

"I didn't get your names," he apologized. "It isn't, by any crazy chance, De Hueck?"

"That is the name," Boris said. "I am the Baron Boris de Hueck. This is my wife, Catherine."

"Well I'll be darned," exclaimed the other. "I just caught a glimpse of that signet ring on your finger and I thought I was daffy. Then I took a good look, and it was my own crest. I'm Walter de Hueck."

"Not our American uncle?" Boris shouted.

Walter de Hueck laughed, and shook hands with Boris.

"So that's what you call me, eh? Yes, I'm the American uncle. And am I glad to see you both! Russian refugees — and my own relatives! You'll stay with us, of course. Me and Ebba. We have a big house in Mayfair, plenty of room, and — but wait until I phone Ebba. She'll be tickled to death."

Walter had spent nine years in Washington at the Russian embassy. He had been transferred to London during the war; but hadn't been in that city long enough to shed all his Americanisms.

"By the way," he said, after he had talked to his wife, "we're printing some money for Wrangle's army. I need a man to take charge of that, Boris, and you are just the man. And you, Catherine, maybe you could make yourself invaluable as a secretary to one of our technical advisers. He can't teach these English girls to speak or understand Russian. Heaven sent you here."

One miracle had happened. Catherine was sure the second would follow.

She knelt in the Chapel of Our Lady of Zion, on Nottingham Hill, and promised that if she became a mother she would dedicate the child to the Virgin-Mother.

From the church she went to a business school and arranged to take courses in typing, shorthand, filing, bookkeeping, and business in general. She meant to be the best stenographer and general secretary in London.

About four months after Uncle Walter came into her life,

Wrangle was defeated. The embassy closed. And Uncle Walter and Aunt Ebba went to the ancestral seat of the De Huecks at Ravel.

Boris and Catherine located an apartment in Earl Square; and Catherine managed to find a job as a stenographer.

"The pay was bad," she says, "but I must admit it was more than I was worth. To my dismay I discovered I was a very poor stenographer, in spite of everything I had done to make myself a good one."

On a Saturday afternoon, with her wages in her purse, and gratitude in her heart because she had not been discharged, she went to see a physician. She had put on her best clothes — Uncle Walter's gift — and so, she thought, had London. The city had never looked so wonderful, nor so kind.

The doctor scoffed at her.

"Madame," he said, "you have a slight cold. Nothing else."

Catherine started to protest, but the specialist silenced her.

"I have made as thorough an examination as medical science permits," he said. "It would be impossible for you to bear a child, or even to conceive. You have a cold. Good day, Madame."

She returned to him a few weeks later. The air was raw and chill, and a fog was rolling in through Harley Street. But she was radiant. And sure.

"It is impossible," the doctor said. "But it is true. Contrary to science, you are going to become a mother. Evidently things that cannot happen, do happen to you."

She went to a department store, and walked dreamily through the aisles, looking at baby clothes, folding rubber bathtubs, toys, and the special foods an infant must be fed.

"Where shall I get money enough?" she wondered.

"God will provide it," was her answer to her own question.

Yet she was frightened. Maybe she was only presuming on God's goodness and mercy. There must be thousands and thousands of other women all over the world as poor as she, and as frightened about the expense. Would God take care of them too?

No wonder many women hesitated at the thought of bearing children. No wonder they said, "I can't afford it." No wonder they practiced birth control, or asked some doctor to take the baby before it could be born.

"If only I could help these poor women," she thought. She said a silent prayer for them, and started down the stairway.

She doesn't know what made her fall. She remembers merely that she tumbled down the long flight to the bottom, and woke up in her apartment to see the specialist glaring at her, and to hear him scold her.

"Madame, through your carelessness, you have almost lost your child. Had you been an ordinary female you would most certainly have lost it — and broken your neck as well. Still, even you have limits. You must lie flat on your back for the rest of your time. Under no circumstances must you get up, unless you wish to murder the baby it was impossible for you to have."

It was agony to lie still all day and all night, and to worry about everything. And it seemed "so unjust."

"I was praying to you, almighty Lord," she complained, "not for myself so much as for all the other poor women in the world. And You let me fall like that! Now I have no job, no hope of getting any money at all. Maybe we'll starve, Lord. And I suffer such constant pain!"

She was heartily ashamed of herself the next moment. God permitted evil only that good might come of it. Not to trust Him fully was a heinous crime. And to question Him? . . .

"God, forgive me!"

He who noted the sparrow's fall would not forsake her. And the pain?

"Your Son knew pain too, pinned to the hard wood of the cross. He offered up that pain for the salvation of the world. Why can I not offer You this little pain that is mine — for all the poor women of the world, and in slight reparation for my sins?"

Hardly had she made this offering than Dunia appeared.

"I've come to stay," she said. "I'll take care of you night and day."

"Where is Boris?" Catherine asked.

"He said he was going to find a job," Dunia answered. "He didn't look well, but I couldn't reason with him. He left just after the doctor came."

"He is still sick," Catherine said, and went to sleep.

Boris found employment, finally. As an architect and an engineer, the graduate of a good school in Russia, he learned that he was eligible to join the leading association of architects in London. Through this organization he was offered work as a landscape architect for a firm in Toronto, Canada.

He came home dispirited.

"Toronto," he said. "Canada. Thousands of miles away. The only job available to me in the entire world. And no way of getting there — especially with you so sick."

"It is the answer to prayer; it is the voice of God," Catherine cried. "He wants us to go to Canada. So, we'll go."

"But you cannot leave your bed!"

"I can lie as flat on my back aboard a ship crossing the Atlantic as I can here," she assured him. "We must go. Canada's climate is like Russia's. We'll feel at home there. God is very good. I still have a jewel or two that will pay our passage."

Less than three months after her fall, Catherine was carried out of the little flat on a stretcher, placed in an ambulance, put aboard a train for Southampton, and taken aboard the small Canadian Pacific liner, *Minnedosa*.

Dunia came along. Boris arranged that. Catherine never learned the details. Boris and Catherine had applied for British citizenship and permission to reside in Canada. The permission was granted, in recognition of their services at Murmansk, and citizenship was promised.

"We traveled as Mr. and Mrs. B. Hook," Catherine says, "Hook being the English equivalent of Hueck. It was a rough passage. We lost a screw from the propeller and the ship rolled abominably. But I was taken out of the tiny cabin below and brought up to the royal suite, and I had a nurse who attended me night and day. I didn't mind the rough weather. Boris, however, had to remain in the hold.

"When we reached St. Johns, New Brunswick, reporters and photographers came aboard to see not Mr. and Mrs. Hook, but the Baron and Baroness de Hueck. We were the first Russian refugees to reach Canada, it seems, so we were 'News.' The reporters said they had heard of our 'thrilling adventures,' and wanted details.

"I suspect the press agent of the steamship line had told the newspapers all these things; though, at the time, I had no idea what a press agent was. I suspect it was he also who arranged for the big reception given us at Toronto, the beautiful flowers, the luncheon, and the speeches of welcome. God bless him.

"I didn't like the publicity at first. But later I was more than grateful for it, because people all over Canada and the United States began to send me all the baby clothes I needed — and all the other things I didn't expect, such as a crib, a play pen, heaps of toys, and a number of folding rubber bathtubs.

"After a few weeks in Canada I felt so well that I thought I could disregard the London specialist's orders. I got up, dressed, and went out to look at Toronto.

"I was all right until I fainted on the street.

"Then there was more publicity, and more things for the baby. I had enough to supply a lot of other mothers.

"My son was born in the Toronto General Hospital, on July 17, 1921, and was christened George Theodore Mario. He was a healthy, normal baby. And with what gratitude I dedicated him to the holy Mother of God."

They had been living in furnished apartments, but after the birth of the baby they bought a modest little house on Nairn Avenue. That is, Catherine explains, they made a down payment, put their signatures on a number of papers, and moved hopefully in. Eventually they moved, unhopefully, out.

"I loved that place," Catherine says. "I loved to make it attractive. I loved washing the dishes, preparing the meals, and working in the garden. It meant more to me than the big house in Petrograd to which I had come as a bride."

After a few months the De Huecks began to feel at home in Canada, to be an integral part of the country. At the same time Catherine felt it her duty, and her privilege, to make good Canadians of her Russian friends.

The publicity she had received attracted many English-speaking Russians to her. Refugees like herself. Her home became a sort of headquarters for them; and she became, before she realized it, the leader of the Russian colony.

Some of the refugees brought news of long lost friends and relatives. And letters came from abroad. Broken threads were gradually knit together. Feasts were held in celebration that somebody dear was still alive. Masses were offered up for the souls of those reported dead.

Life was peaceful and gay, until Boris became too sick to continue working, and Catherine felt she must once more become the breadwinner. She had no trouble this time getting work.

She sent in her card to the man in charge of personnel at the T. Eaton & Co. store.

"Baroness Catherine de Hueck."

The gentleman didn't keep his distinguished visitor waiting. He emerged from his sanctum smiling a welcome, anxious to be of service.

"It is an honor to serve you, Baroness," he said. "A great honor. What can I do for you?"

"I want a job," the Baroness said sweetly.

The gentleman gasped for breath.

"I speak many languages," Catherine said. "I think I would be invaluable in your mail order department. You must get letters from French, Russian, and German people."

"Baroness," he said, "you are, from the hour of 8 o'clock tomorrow morning, an employee of the store. Let me escort you to the mail order department now."

On her way home Catherine had an idea. She could teach French. She was teaching several Russian women to speak and read English. She had discovered she was a good teacher. She got no money from these women. They were her friends, and they were very poor. But, if she could get pupils for French lessons, at say two dollars an hour, she might be able to double the salary the store had promised.

She went to 5:30 o'clock Mass every morning. There usually was no altar boy to serve this Mass. Sometimes Catherine would kneel just outside the altar rail, make the responses, and ring the little bell.

But after she went to work in the store all this was changed.

"I still went to early Mass," she says, "but I was so tired, after working all the day before, then rushing home to get dinner and straighten the house, taking care of the baby and my sick husband, hurrying out to a French lesson, running to the home of some Russian woman to give her a lesson in English, and then going home — maybe to walk the floor with George until 1 or 2 o'clock in the morning — I was so tired that, invariably, I fell asleep in church. I didn't pray. I didn't wake up for Communion. I came out of a deep slumber only when I heard the feet of other worshipers going past me in the aisle. Only my will was partaking of the Mass.

" 'Never mind,' the priest comforted me. 'Perhaps it is God Himself who closes your eyes. He must know how tired you are, how much in need of sleep. Maybe these are the best Masses you ever offered Him, since you give Him the anguish of getting up so early. Don't you think He accepts that? And is there anything wrong in a child's sleeping in her Father's house? Continue to be a little child.'

"After that, naturally, I never could sleep again in church."

Frequently she worked harder for others than she did for herself; getting jobs for them, patching up family quarrels, helping a couple get married, writing letters in English or French for immigrants who didn't know any language but Russian — even cleaning the houses of sick women, and tending the needs of their children.

"At this time," she says, "Canada was taking in many Russian refugees, and farming them out, as it were, until they paid their passage money. For instance, two friends of Boris came to Toronto, aristocratic gentleman who had never done anything in their lives more strenuous than riding a horse. They were, to their horror, sent to the north woods, to work as lumberjacks for eighteen months.

"One of them was in his early thirties, the other a year or so younger. They were thin, sickly, dispirited. They felt they were being sent to the equivalent of the salt mines. And they wished they had stayed in Russia.

"I got letters from them, occasionally. They had been set, at first, to felling trees. They collapsed. Then they were made to trim logs for railroad ties, chop off all the branches, saw them in lengths, and square them roughly with the ax. The worst part of the job was lifting those green logs, after they had been trimmed, and placing them on the freight cars.

"They were so stiff the first night they couldn't move. They couldn't get up the next morning. But the foreman got them up. 'I'll tell you what will take the soreness out of your muscles,' he said. 'More of the same! Get to work!'

"Within two months each of those poor Russians bulged with muscles. He ate enormously, and slept like the dead. He could pick up a log and toss it onto the train without any trouble. And he felt as rich as a king.

"They were getting something like five dollars a day — and, as they lived in the bush, they couldn't spend a penny. When they came back to Toronto, after their eighteen months they each had a little fortune — but both wanted to go right back to the woods. One of these men is now an artist, employed in one of the comic strip studios in Hollywood. The other — I've lost track of him.

"The women refugees were farmed out mostly as housemaids. One young aristocrat complained bitterly that her mistress made her clean all the wallpaper in the house.

" 'She makes me use chunks of bread that have been soaked in water,' she told me. 'Bread! And my people dying for lack of bread in Russia. Bread for such a dirty job. And it is so immense a house!' "

For a woman who was an excellent cook, Catherine managed to open a restaurant — enlisting friends to design Russian murals, make Russian costumes for the waitresses, and print menu cards in Russian and English. She succeeded in giving the place a Russian atmosphere, in getting the newspapers interested, and in making the opening night a social event. The receipts of that first night not only paid all the preliminary expenses, but gave the owner substantial working capital.

For another friend, Catherine opened a beauty parlor. For a third, she secured a dress shop. For a dozen others she got jobs in the T. Eaton store.

She was regarded as something of a queen at the time her brother Serge came on a visit.

"You must stay here," Catherine said. "This is the greatest country in the world. I'll get you a job. What would you like to do? We'll bring the whole family here. In a little while . . ."

But all her plans were changed by a letter from Antrea.

Her father had died. And there wasn't much of an estate. The big house, the outbuildings, and what was left of the livestock had to be sold. There wasn't much money in Finland. Few people could buy anything.

Serge had to return to Antrea. Eventually he took his mother and his brother Andrew to Brussels. There was just enough money to establish them in a modest house.

Something of her father's spirit entered into Catherine with the news of his death.

It was not enough to remain in Toronto and earn the little money her work paid. She had two families to support now. She must make a great deal of money. That meant she must go to New York.

"I didn't have any crazy ideas," she says, "such as that the streets of Manhattan were paved with gold; or that it would be ridiculously easy to make money there. But I knew it was the richest and greatest city in the world, and I was sure that, eventually, I could make more money there than I could make anywhere else."

She went to see her parish priest, Father McCabe, pastor of St. Clare's.

"Who is going to look after the baby?" the priest demanded.

"Dunia. She's crazy about George, and there isn't anybody on earth I'd rather trust with him."

"Dunia!" the pastor snorted. "What sort of an outlandish name is that?"

Catherine told him something about the girl. "She became a Catholic after she came here," she added, "and wanted to be a nun. She entered a convent, but became too ill to stay there. When she left the convent she came back to us."

Father McCabe plunged a hand through a rip in his shiny cassock, pulled out some crumpled bills, and put them in Catherine's hands.

"I might know that as soon as I had a little money," he said, "it would be taken from me. Go to New York, Katie. And God bless you."

Catherine needed no further urging.

*   *   *

"There's an Irish way of putting it, that sometimes gets results," Mr. Dee asserted. "Catherine, mavourneen, how wud ye like to be buried with my people?"

"I'd like that," Catherine said. "But — wouldn't I have to be married to you before I could receive the honor you suggest?"

"You would."

"Let's talk of something else then, Mr. Dee."

⚡ 13 ⚡

"ANYTHING can happen in New York," she kept saying as the train brought her close to the great city. "Anything at all."

She fancied she might become a secretary to the president of some big firm in Wall Street. She might become a buyer for a department store, and travel constantly to and from Europe. She might become a great journalist or a famous author.

Ever since she was a little girl she had remembered stories her father had told her about New York, and stories she had read of the city's fascination.

A few days after she had added herself to the millions of inhabitants of the city, she woke from her dreams to find herself a worker in a cheap laundry, and a resident of Ma Murphy's boardinghouse. It was close to the Hudson river, the wailing tugboats, and the great ocean liners.

She was no longer the Queen of Toronto's Russian colony. She was "Katie the Polack." And her pay was only eight dollars a week.

Eight dollars a week! She tried hard, desperately hard, to save something out of that for her son, her sick husband, her mother, and her brothers. But even though she went without food, she had to pay the rent — and there was never more than a dollar to send any one of her dependents.

She organized the laundry girls, and called a strike.

"I have told the story of this strike many times," she says, "not because it is interesting in itself, but merely to point out that the only people who came to help us on the picket line were the Communists.

"Where were the Catholics? I don't know. Perhaps they were in the Waldorfs of America, discussing plans for Catholic charity drives at $2.50 or so a plate. Certainly neither the clergy nor the laity were interested in our fight for a decent wage, or in our pitiful weakness and poverty. It was inconceivable to me that this should be so. Yet it was so. It was inconceivable also that the believers in atheism, the people who had wrecked holy Russia, were the only ones who cared what happened to us. They were there constantly during the strike, with coffee and doughnuts, and sympathy and advice, and even ready cash now and then. They were there, and I began to fear for America."

The strike was lost. Catherine became a waitress, going from one restaurant to another, after the fashion of waitresses. The tips were always better somewhere else — yet they were never enough to support those wretched ones who must be supported. And they were never enough to keep a girl in decent clothes, to pay her room rent, or to give her any sort of luxuries.

Maybe journalism would pay better, Catherine thought. She tried to prepare herself by taking extension courses in journalism, literature, history, short-story writing, and other subjects at Columbia University, and did manage to get a job on the *New York World*.

"I was a sort of leg woman to the society editor," she explains, "but I couldn't bear writing about some debutante's party dress with gold-leaf adjectives. I kept remembering that other girls were walking the streets at night in the hope of getting the price of a hat or a new pair of shoes."

She washed dishes in a greasy-spoon restaurant. She dished

them off the elbow at a cheap lunch counter on the Bowery. She was an assistant cook in a Chinatown place, and part of her job was to provide "atmosphere" for the tourists who came on the sight-seeing buses. She posed as a dumb and sullen creature for the spielers:

"And this, Ladies and Gentlemen, is a white girl captive, raised in China by Mongolian bandits who killed her missionary parents in the north of China. She was brought to this country by a reputable Chinese merchant, who paid a thousand silver dollars for her ransom. She speaks not a word of English, and understands only one of the many Chinese dialects. She is gently treated here, we are assured, but evidently she still remembers her tragic childhood. She has never been known to smile."

Once in a while, once in a great while, some elderly woman would thrust a nickel or a dime into the white captive's hands, and once a young woman gave her a quarter.

Sometimes, after working all day in a restaurant, she would dance all night in a Greenwich Village cabaret. She made her own costumes, and chose her own dancing partners from among the other Russian refugees in New York.

"We danced for our dinners," she says, "and for such fun as we could find in the work. We were seldom paid."

There were times when she had no job, when she couldn't find anything. But she never quite despaired. If she had had no breakfast, she was confident she would have lunch. If she had had neither breakfast nor lunch she looked forward, confidently, to a good dinner.

"There were glorious nights even in the most terrible weeks," she says, "such as the evening I went to visit a cabaret in the Village to see if I could arrange to dance there with a partner."

A man was singing as she approached the door, singing in Russian, singing in a voice she knew and loved, singing in a voice that stopped her and shook her.

She remained just outside the door until the singing ended, homesickness flooding all her veins. Then she walked slowly into the room. The lights hurt her eyes. The smoke and the warmth of the place hit her like a blow. She could see no one she recognized. Had she been listening to a voice on the radio?

Then she saw him. Chaliapin! A tall, wide, powerful stevedore towering above the bar. He was standing like an emperor, and drinking like a moujik.

He saw the girl staring at him, and cried out so that the walls shook.

"A Russian! A Russian beauty from the steppes!"

He bowed low to her. He took her hand and led her to a table.

"A beauty!" he repeated. "Look at those eyes, blue as the Volga. Look at that blonde hair, glorious as the birch leaves in October. Look at that forehead, wide and mysterious and lovely as the very steppes. Little Russian girl, I will sing to you. I will sing to you alone."

He sang song after song, filling his golden throat with liquor after each melody. And suddenly the night was done.

"Run home, little child from the Volga," the great singer thundered, "or my heart will break with the beauty and the tragedy you bring back to me out of the New York night."

A woman followed Catherine as she went out. She was clutching Chaliapin's fur hat to her bosom.

"How fortunate you are," she cried. "How blessed! The greatest man in the world has sung to you for an hour. Never forget this night."

Catherine walked away from the Village, and found a Greek restaurant open. She obtained a job as dishwasher, a cup of lukewarm coffee, and a bite of underdone hamburger. She walked a mile to her room, and dreamed all night of a prince who sang to her.

She worked in the restaurant until the following Saturday.

"We're going to Coney Island over the week end," the proprietor informed her when she asked for her pay. "You won't need any money."

"I am spending the week end alone," Catherine said.

"No Coney Island?"

Catherine shook her head.

"No Coney Island, no pay."

Catherine put on her hat and coat and walked out. She went to her room. The landlady met her in the hallway.

"I'm sorry," Catherine said, "I have no money. I cannot pay you tonight."

"No pay, no room," the landlady said.

Catherine walked aimlessly through New York.

"There's nothing new in this story," she says. "It is so hackneyed not even the worst amateur writer would use it. But it was not at all hackneyed to me. I had no job. I had no money. I had no place on which to lay my head.

"For hours I tramped the streets looking for work. There was no work of any kind. I paused outside a convent. I determined to ask for shelter there. And I was sure I should be welcomed.

"I have told this story, also, many times. I have told it especially to nuns. It may be hackneyed, too, but it will never be hackneyed to me. It is the story of one of the events that shaped my life. I tell it without any bitterness. I tell it even against my will. It is a story that must be told.

"I went to the door of the convent and rang the bell. I waited. For many minutes I waited, cold and hungry and weak. It was all I could do to stand up. A sweet-faced Sister opened the door, just a little, and looked at me as though I were some sort of monster.

" 'Sister,' I said, 'I am a Catholic. I have lost my home. I have no money. I have no place to stay. I am hungry and tired and cold. May I come in? May I stay here overnight?'

" 'You have come to the wrong place,' the nun told me. 'What you want is the Catholic Charities.'

"She started to close the door.

" 'Where is that, Sister?' I asked.

"She did not know exactly, but said I would have no difficulty finding it.

" 'But even so,' I pointed out, 'surely they will not be open at this time of night. Maybe they will not open until Monday. Must I keep walking all that time — or sleep in Central Park?'

" 'I am sorry,' the Sister said, 'but I have no right to let you in.'

"She closed the door in my face.

"No, I don't like to tell that story. But I must. There are hundreds of girls who find themselves in my fix and who go to the Sisters for help. There should be a place for them in every convent; a bed for everyone of Christ's little ones; some Christian help to keep them from the temptations and the dangers that followed me that night.

"I walked on in a daze. There had been a cross on that convent, the cross of the gentle Saviour who had said, 'Come to Me all ye who are heavy laden.' I had come to Him; and by His own spouse I had been turned away."

She walked downtown, mile after weary mile. On the Bowery she saw a Name in electric lights, a Name that brought joy to her anguish, and strength to her weary limbs. The holy Name of Jesus!

She almost ran to it, with prayers of thanks in her heart and on her lips. L trains roared above the street. Drunks reeled close to her on the sidewalk. Men and women slumming, pushed and shoved her. Newsboys shouted in her ears. Taxis honked. Great trucks roared by. A policeman whistled shrilly at the traffic. But all she saw was that Name in the electric lights.

But when she came close to the sign she saw that it said, "Jesus Saves."

Unconsciously her feet slowed, her resolution faltered. She looked at the building and hesitated a long time before she entered its door. Why should the place that flaunted so glorious a Name look so shabby, so forbidding, so desolate and cold?

In a small room at the top of a dark, ill-smelling stairway, she found a group of men and women. The men were sitting on old and rickety chairs on one side of the room. The women sat on the other side, in chairs equally decrepit. A severe-looking woman was talking to them about hell and damnation.

Catherine seated herself with the women and listened. She was shocked that such things should be preached to the poor and the hungry. Why could not that woman have talked about the love of God, the mercy of God, the joy of heaven?

Eventually the woman ended her sermon, looked at Catherine critically and with evident suspicion, and began to question her. In the few moments since her entrance, Catherine had learned what was expected of her. She must make herself subservient, humble, and exceedingly grateful.

The woman talked acidly of Catherine "and her kind," spoke

of prostitutes, and let it be known that she had only a loathing and a contempt and a holy hatred for such creatures — as became a decent Christian woman.

Catherine bowed her head and chose a moment of silence to ask if she might have something to eat.

"This is a Christian place," the woman said sternly. "We turn no one away hungry, though their sins be as scarlet."

She whisked away, to return in a moment, with a cup of cold, muddy coffee, and one small doughnut.

When Catherine had finished her supper she was led to a shower, and told to remove her clothes, that they might be sterilized. She was given a bar of coarse strong soap and told to scrub her body thoroughly. Another woman stood by to see she obeyed that order. Then she was given a gray prickly nightgown, two prickly blankets, and a cot down the hall.

She fell asleep instantly, to be awakened at 4:30 o'clock in the morning by a woman shaking her roughly.

"Up," the woman shouted. "Up and out."

Catherine and her companions were given their clothes and let out into the street without breakfast, without a chance to wash, without a friendly word or smile.

She stood on the sidewalk a long time, looking up at the sign, "Jesus Saves." The lights had gone out.

It was drizzling. And it was still cold. Catherine walked up the Bowery toward the Brooklyn Bridge, and, for the second time in her life, thought seriously of suicide. She walked out on the bridge and looked at the dark, cold river.

"No," she said aloud.

She walked back to the Bowery, and started uptown. Somewhere on Broadway she saw an all-night hamburger joint. She stood in front of the lighted window, trying to warm herself by the light, trying to fill her starving body with the sight and the smell of frying meat, trying to nerve herself to go inside and ask for a hamburger and a job. Her nose was flat against the pane and her breath was blurring the glass when she became aware that someone was calling to her.

She turned around.

"You. Blonde goil. You hungry?"

He was a little man, dark, shabby, but smiling. He was a taxi driver, sitting in his car at the curb.

"Yeah," Catherine said. "I'm hungry."

"You be interested in a hamboiga?"

They sat close together on two stools before the counter almost before Catherine was aware of the fact.

"Don't be ascared of me, goily," the taxi driver said. "I got a kid about your age. Eat hearty. It's all on me, and you don' owe me nuttin'."

She ate four hamburgers and drank three cups of coffee. Then she went outside into the cold drizzle while the taxi man stopped at the cashier's desk.

"Now I'll have to pay," Catherine thought. She wasn't indignant. She wasn't afraid. It just didn't seem to matter.

"Got a home, goily?" the taxi driver asked her.

"No."

"I t'ought so. How's about comin' home with me? Boidy'll give you a room. Boidy's the frau. A great kid. You'll like her. Get in the cab and we'll go. I was knockin' off work anyway, and just goin' home when I get a gander at you tryin' to inhale a hamboig through the glass."

He did have a wife and a daughter in his little home on the east side. And they were as good to Catherine as the head of the house had been.

They had a second breakfast at his home, and the taxi driver put on his hat and bent his head before the meal — which made Catherine think of another Jew who had been kind to all who came His way.

She had a warm bath, a long sleep, a dinner of gefüllte fish, and then another long sleep. After breakfast, on Monday morning, the taxi driver loaned her enough money to pay her landlady, and to live for another week.

⇛ 14 ⇚

SHE sat on a bench in Madison Square, a tiny valley hemmed in by skyscrapers, and spent an hour in rest and meditation. She was out of a job again, and weary with walking the streets in quest of another.

This was what she needed, she thought, this peaceful bit of the country, these people who walked so leisurely by, these children who played with such innocent joy on the new grass, these birds dependent only upon God.

She must get away from New York for a little time. She must go to the country where Christ walked every morning. She must build up her strength and her confidence, and then come back. But how could she do that? And where could she go?

She watched a baby plucking off the bright yellow heads of the dandelions, and remembered a child lying under a tree on the top of a little hill in Finland and dreaming of the future.

"God help me and mine," she prayed.

A gust of wind blew a sheet of newspaper toward her, and wrapped it around her ankle. She lifted it and found an answer to her prayer. A family in Long Island wanted an upstairs maid. She tore out the ad, thrust it into her pocketbook, and walked to the Long Island depot.

An affable woman, the mistress of the mansion, questioned her at length, and hired her without a reference. Catherine liked her. She liked the house. She liked the other servants. The pay was good, and the work ridiculously easy.

She had plenty of time to herself, time for long walks in the countryside, time for study, time for prayer and meditation, and time to worry about all those dear to her.

"It was like a retreat," Catherine describes this time. "The cook was a pleasant Irish woman and a devout Catholic. Some of the maids and two of the chauffeurs were also Catholics, and we said the rosary every night in the kitchen — the cleanest and brightest and coziest kitchen in the universe. The butler was an Englishman, and an Episcopalian, but he was in love with the cook, so he joined in the rosary with us every night."

One of the chauffeurs was a Connaughtman, not long out of the auld sod; a sensible young man with an eye for beauty. Catherine hadn't been in the house for a week before he suggested she become his wife.

"Sure, Lass," he said, "let us both save our money, ivery penny of it, get married, and go back to Europe. We'll take service with some great family and live like a lady and a lord. You know well, Katie, we can live like the gentry themselves, and raise the childer dacintly. Sure now, do they grow up here, it's whiskey flasks they will be toting on their hips before they are sixteen, God save them, and staying out till all hours — and in them fast cars they make these days. Wurra, wurra, this is no place at all, at all, to bring up children."

"You're a fine man, Pat," Catherine answered, "but for lands' sake don't talk like that to me. Marriage isn't for me. And don't ask me why."

"Marriage," said Pat, "is for all women who do not want to be nuns. Is it a vocation you have, Katie? Then don't let the likes of me tempt you from it."

Catherine would have stayed in this mansion, "indefinitely," she says, had it not been for the family who owned the place.

"They were good people in their way," she explains, "they treated us kindly, they were considerate, they were generous; but they led such empty and dissolute lives, had such worldly and futile ambitions. Their chief aim in life was to get themselves accepted by New York society."

Two incidents quickened her intention of returning to the battle of New York.

Walking through the parlor one afternoon on her way to the kitchen she surprised the daughter of the house sitting on the lap of a handsome young visitor. The girl looked up and saw the upstairs maid, but did not alter her position.

"It's only one of the servants," she said in French to her boy friend. "Don't be alarmed, my dear."

The next day one of the waitresses was ill, and Catherine was asked to take her place at dinner. That evening the French teacher, who was indoctrinating Mama, her daughter, and her son, in the niceties of the language as it was spoken in the salons of Paris, was a guest at the table.

She stared at Catherine as she carried in the soup tureen, and turned to Mama with an outburst of French.

"That girl is much too young and beautiful to have in this house, if you ask me." She leered. "If I were the mother of such a handsome young son as yours, Madame, I'd be afraid of her."

Years after Catherine left this mansion she met Mama again. It was at a luncheon in the Plaza Hotel. Catherine was the principal speaker on the program, and occupied the seat of honor. Madame came forward begging to be introduced.

"I have heard so much about the wonderful Baroness de Hueck," she said, "and I have been just dying to meet you!

I've been admiring your gown, and your adorable hat. And those Parma violets. Where does one get such violets at this time of the year? And for the last half hour I have been wondering if we haven't met before. Your face is so familiar!"

Catherine almost said, "You once hired me as an upstairs maid in your home in Long Island," but she feared that might embarrass the gushing socialite.

"Oh," she said, "all Russians look alike. You have probably met many of us."

She stayed only a few months in the Long Island retreat, then found a job selling perfumes and cosmetics in Macy's.

She told nobody that she was a baroness; but, because of her accent, her stately carriage, and her European outlook on current events, the girls dubbed her "the princess."

When the customers learned that she was "a real Russian princess, a refugee," her sales increased. Many women thought it was "wonderful" to be waited on by a noblewoman. Some insisted on knowing if she had ever seen Rasputin, and one or two wanted to know all about the private lives of the Czar and the Czarina.

To one friendly woman Catherine spoke freely.

"I did see Rasputin once," she said, "but from a distance. And I did see the Czar and his family. But not formally. They came into the Hall of the Nobility, in Petrograd, one November afternoon, where I had a booth, selling knickknacks for charity. This was a yearly custom, this charity bazaar, which was dear to all the Russian noble families.

"The hall in which the bazaar was held was as big as the Grand Central depot, and there were booths everywhere. We sold all kinds of things, and the imperial family came to buy. They came slowly down the aisles, the Czar, the Czarina, the young Czarevnas, and the Czarevitch, with all their attendants — a little army. They stopped now and then, and the Czar and Czarina chatted with this noblewoman or that. And at every booth the Czar left ten gold rubles.

"My Aunt Vera had a big booth. I had a tiny one, adjoining hers. The Czar and Czarina stopped to speak to my aunt. They didn't notice me. I was only a child. But the Princess Tatyana winked at me, and I winked at her. She smiled, and I smiled. We were about the same age, thirteen or fourteen.

"When the imperial party moved on, Tatyana lingered behind. At my booth.

" 'It must be exciting to sell things,' she said.

" 'It is,' I told her.

" 'You must have lots of fun. A czarevna never has any fun at all. Life is a bore. What is your name?'

" 'Katia.'

" 'Katia, do you mind if I help you sell, before they find out I am missing?'

"I made room for her, smiling. Everybody who had seen her enter my booth crowded around, eager to buy from her. There must have been two hundred people there, and more were coming all the time.

" 'Look, Katia,' the princess cried, 'I'm selling. I'm making change. I'm having fun!'

" 'And you are cleaning out my booth fast, Your Royal Highness,' I answered, 'and I shall get the prize. Thank you.'

"Even as we talked frightened men and women were searching for Tatyana all over the great hall. But my booth was empty of every knickknack when they found her and took her away.

"I met her again, a few years later, when I came home on leave from the front. It was in the Red Cross headquarters in

Petrograd. She was rolling bandages. She called me to her and exclaimed over me:

" 'Oh, Katia,' she said, 'you have been to the front! And you have been decorated with the St. George Medal! How I envy you! You have really lived, Katia. You have been blessed.'

" 'And you, Your Royal Highness?' I asked.

" 'Life is still a bore to me,' she said.

"A few months later she was murdered with the others of her family."

There were tears in the eyes of the friendly woman when Catherine finished her story. "I must ask a favor of you," she said. "I have some guests coming for luncheon at my home to-morrow. It's a holiday, and you don't have to work, do you? I would be so honored if you would come."

There were about twenty people at the luncheon, and they began bombarding Catherine with questions even before they sat down to eat. The next day one of the guests came to the perfume counter and asked for a few moments.

"I don't want to buy anything," she said. "I want to sell you something."

"If you can sell me something you are good," Catherine said.

"I want to sell you the idea of going on the Chautauqua circuit. I can guarantee you one hundred dollars a week for at least six months."

"One hundred dollars a week?"

The woman nodded her head.

"I'll let you know tomorrow," Catherine said.

The rest of the day passed by itself. Catherine didn't push it at all. She remained at the moment when she heard she could earn one hundred dollars a week. She was too weak and too flustered to do anything about the time.

Sometime that evening she went to the phone and called a Franciscan priest. She asked him about the Chautauqua circuit, and demanded to know if there was anything immoral about it.

"What makes you think there is?" the priest inquired.

"They are going to pay me one hundred dollars a week, Father," Catherine explained. "Surely it must be immoral."

The priest laughed uproariously. He tried to talk, but he kept interrupting himself with his own laughter; so that it was a long time before Catherine realized she had nothing to worry about.

"My child," the priest assured her, "the Chautauqua is one of the most moral institutions in this most moral country. You just get up and talk, then move on and talk some more. You will never damn your immortal soul on the Chautauqua circuit, even at a hundred dollars a week."

"But, Father, what will I talk about?" Catherine said.

The priest was still laughing when he hung up.

On her way home Catherine stopped for a long time at St. Patrick's Cathedral, giving thanks that a new life had dawned for her and those so sorely dependent on her.

⇛ 15 ⇚

"WHAT shall I talk about?" Catherine asked the Chautauqua manager.

"Russia," he said. "Tell the same stories you have been telling to your friends."

"And may I talk about Communism, and the danger it holds for the world?"

"Naturally. But make it interesting. Don't try to use correct English, or people may think you an impostor. Stick to that lovely accent you use in ordinary talk. It not only stamps you as the real thing, but it does something to people."

"And where do we start?"

"Sudbury."

"In Canada?"

"Yes, in Canada. I hope you do not mind."

It seemed a little too much to believe. She was not only to earn real money, she was given an opportunity to fight the Communists, and she would see Canada again and all that Canada meant to her.

She spent a number of days in Toronto, discussing the miracle of fortune with Boris and Dunia and Father McCabe and other friends, sewing the costume she would wear, and making plans for the distribution of her weekly pay.

"There was only one black cloud on my horizon," Catherine says, "but it was so huge and so ugly and so terrifying, that for many hours it obscured everything else in my life.

"That cloud made itself felt on the day before we opened in Sudbury. I suddenly remembered that I must stand up and speak to a vast audience, to intelligent people, and I must keep talking to them for an hour or so. In my excitement and elation over the change in my life and what it would mean for my people, I had forgotten that I must face an audience and make them like me.

"Cold sweat poured out of me when I fully realized that I was supposed to be a lecturer. The only times I had ever talked in public I had spoken to soldiers gathered around a field kitchen. And it hadn't mattered much what I said to them.

"I couldn't eat. I couldn't sleep. I lived in torture all night, and all the next day. When the ordeal came at last, when I was introduced to my first audience and stepped out onto the platform, I was pale and cold. I tried to smile, but my face was frozen. I looked at the hundreds of people sitting in rows before me, but for several minutes I couldn't think of a word to say.

"Then I began to tell the story of my life, as I had told it to people in London, in Toronto, and in New York.

"You remember the old Chautauqua days? The big tent? Cows mooing and children screaming and shouting just outside the canvas? Autos backfiring now and then? Mules braying? And maybe a long freight train going by not far away?

"I found, somewhat to my surprise, that I could make myself heard in the last row of seats, despite all the disturbing noises outside the tent; and I gave thanks to God that I had learned the art in the days when I shouted at the troops.

"Halfway through my story I began to cry. I was talking of my father at the time, but I wasn't weeping because of his death. I was weeping through sheer nervousness and a sleepless night and the thought that nobody here in Canada could possibly be interested in what had happened to a girl in distant Russia so many years before.

"I couldn't stop crying. And, strange to say, hundreds of people started crying with me. Some furtively wiped their eyes. Some sat still and let the tears stream down their cheeks. Some sobbed unashamed. A few almost strangled in their grief.

"When I had finished my story and had left the stage, the audience sat still and stiff, and I had visions of going back to Macy's and asking for my old job.

"But the manager came rushing to greet me. And there was ecstasy in his face. 'Wonderful!' he said. 'Magnificent! Incredible!'

"While I was wondering which of us was crazy, the silent people came to life with a thunder of applause that grew and grew. I had to go back to the stage and bow again and again.

" 'I never saw anything like it,' the manager assured me. 'You are a hit, a tremendous hit. Can you cry every night?'

" 'No,' I said, 'of course not.'

" 'I'll put onions in your handkerchief.'

" 'No.'

" 'I'll give you $150 a week.'

" 'No.'

" 'I'll give you $300 a week.'

"I became hysterical. I rushed away from him. I knew I could not cry again, and would not, and should not, even for $300 a week."

The Chautauqua moved on. All over Canada. All over the United States. It visited the little towns and villages, the remote hamlets, the regions never reached by theatrical road shows or circuses or fairs.

The lecturers spoke in the afternoon, 360 afternoons a year. There was a theatrical performance in the evening. When it was finished, and while the audiences were streaming out of the tent, and the canvas was being pulled down, the artists got into their cars and started for the next town on the circuit.

There was always a ride through dark, narrow, winding roads, many of them unpaved. Eight passenger cars took the lecturers and "the other talent," the singers, musicians, and players; and one of them drove while the others tried to sleep.

"Tonight," says Catherine, "there would be a bad hotel, bad food, a hard bed. Cheer up. It will be worse tomorrow. Make the best of tonight."

Six months after she went on the circuit her salary had been tripled, and she had not wept again — at least not before her audiences. For nearly three years she lived this life; and during part of it she doubled as an actress, playing the maid in *Seventh Heaven,* a very small role. She was given the part when the regular player went to a hospital.

"I earned every penny of the $40,000 or more I made in those years," Catherine says, "and ended with a nervous and physical breakdown that lasted six months. Where I went in those months, what I did, how I lived, I do not remember. All I remember of this period is becoming aware that I had no money, and that all my dependents were in sore need. I had to go back to the grind again.

"I returned to the lecture platform, but not to the Chautauqua. I went on tour for the Leigh-Emmerich Lecture Bureau, one of the biggest agencies in the country, and again I was given $300 a week.

"The strain was just as great, though we visited only the big cities on this circuit. I found I could be just as tired in Chicago, Denver, San Francisco, or Minneapolis, as in any small community; could find just as hard a bed and just as indigestible a dinner. After a few years I had to quit again.

" 'That's all right,' Mr. Emmerich said. 'You can't go on forever talking about the Communists. I know you have to quit, but don't quit me. How would you like to go abroad and buy talent for the bureau?"

" 'Abroad? You mean Europe?'

" 'England, France, Germany, Italy, the Balkans — wherever you have to go to dig up good lecturers.'

" 'Belgium too?'

" 'That's where your mother is, eh?'

" 'My mother and my brothers. You mean I'll actually have a chance to see them again?'

" 'And how! I'll give you $125 a week, a bonus — depending on how and what you deliver — and all your traveling expenses, of course. Before long, if you are as good as I think you are, you'll be making more than $300 a week. What do you say?'

"I said 'Gosh,' and hurried to St. Patrick's to thank God."

≫ 16 ≪

AS THE big liner went down the Hudson, Catherine turned her thoughts from the city she was leaving — New York where anything can happen, where a girl can starve, where a laundry worker can become a famous lecturer, and a foreigner can become a real American — and looked forward with excitement to the easy ways of Europe.

The long noon hour. The chocolate of France. The tea of England. The leisurely luncheons and unhurried dinners. The feeling of relaxation in the transaction of business. The bargaining with shopkeepers. The long discussions over art or music or literature in the sunshine of a sidewalk café.

Yet, before she had been a week in Europe, she was rushing around as though she were still in the United States, and bragging to old friends about American efficiency, American pep, American speed, American production, American service, and American ideas.

"It was impossible for my mother to realize I had grown up," she says, "and difficult beyond all telling for her to believe I was making an honest living. There was hanky-panky somewhere in my job, she was sure. *Schaharie-maharie.* Dirty work at the crossroads. She translated my dollar wages into Belgian francs — thousands and thousands of them. That was hard enough for her to digest. But the fact that all my expenses were being paid she simply could not swallow.

" 'Nobody in his senses,' she insisted, 'is going to send a hare-

132

brained girl to Europe, and give her a million francs or more just to spend!' "

And the elder lady objected strenuously to Catherine's male companions.

"Why do you go out so much with that American?" she would ask.

"He's a friend I met in New York. He has his own yacht and gives a lot of parties aboard it. And there's nothing wrong with my going anywhere with him, unescorted. American women never have escorts when they go out with men."

Catherine's mother was bewildered.

"Why don't you go out with Serge's friend?" she once asked. "He's a much better man than any of your friends. He's a brilliant student. He's a gentleman. He's a Catholic. He doesn't say 'Hi, Babe' to me. He doesn't wear loud clothes, and he speaks four languages instead of trying to speak only one."

At the time Catherine saw nothing unique in her mother's preference for the student, though he was an extremely black Congo prince. It was only after she had become engaged in the Negro apostolate in American cities, and had discovered the prejudice that exists against colored people, that she attached any significance to her mother's preference.

Catherine made her headquarters with her mother in Brussels, and traveled by plane or train or boat, to Ostend, Lisbon, Salamanca, London, Paris, Nice, Oslo, Berlin, Munich, Dublin, or Prague — wherever a potential lecturer might be unearthed.

There were lunches and dinners with eminent authors and celebrities of all kinds, and with people who might put the talent scout in close contact with her prey.

Cables from Emmerich spurred her on.

"Must get Arnold Bennett. Money no object."

She tracked down Bennett and took him to dine.

"If you want lecturer who stutters," she cabled New York, "you can have Bennett."

The answer was contained in one word. "Cancel."

Galsworthy, Philip Gibbs, William McFee, G. K. Chesterton, Hilaire Belloc, Liam O'Flaherty, Margaret Kennedy, Virginia Woolf, Leon Feuchtwanger, André Maurois, Lady Margaret Sackville, G. B. Stern, Radcliffe Hall, Lothrop Stoddard, F. Brett Young, Cyril Joad, Bertrand Russell, Sheila Kaye-Smith, J. B. Priestley, Aldous Huxley — the list of her prospective clients embraced all these and many others. Some she signed up on the dotted line, others she failed to interest.

In London, an American woman who had married a title and joined the horsy set, invited Catherine to a dinner where she met thirty or more of the celebrities she was hunting.

After the dessert the conversation took a metaphysical trend, and almost everyone of those distinguished writers, artists, and professors declared there was no God.

The hostess then, spitefully perhaps, called attention to the one believer at the table.

"We have in our midst a very charming young woman who still lives in the middle ages, though she hurries like winged lightning through the cities of modern Europe. She not only believes in God but goes to church every morning of her life. The Baroness de Hueck, my friends, is an ardent Catholic, a super Catholic. A daily communicant. Wouldn't it be interesting to hear what she has to say?"

"Bravo," everybody cried, even those who had been loudest in their conviction of atheism. "Bravo, let's hear from the charming Catholic."

Catherine thought to herself: "There go all my contracts; there goes my job."

But she stood up, and — at first shyly, then with gusto, and finally with all the vigor of her heart and all the tricks of her lecturer's lungs — she talked of Father, Son, and Holy Ghost.

Before she, or anyone else, realized it, she was preaching a sermon on the various talents God gave to His servants, and the way to develop those talents.

"You did not make yourself great," she challenged each one. "You had something to start with. You had a talent given you by God. You developed that talent by study and work. But if God had not given you that talent, all your work, and all your study would have been of no avail. And you can never perfect that talent unless you have the love and the help of the Master. Thank God for what He has so generously given you. He didn't have to give it, remember. And you can lose it easily. Thank God, and learn to love Him. For the more you love Him, the more He will help you. That's common sense."

She sat down abruptly, feeling she had made herself the most unpopular young woman in all the British empire. And everybody crowded around her to shake her hands, to kiss her, to ask a hundred questions, and to demand lunch and dinner dates!

There were a number of other talent seekers in London who were desperately trying to meet Catherine's lunch and dinner hosts and hostesses, but could not get them even to answer letters.

"How do you do it?" one of them asked her.

Catherine pretended not to understand.

"How do you manage to get so close to people like Lytton Strachey or Bertrand Russell, for instance, and other writers who do not know that the rest of us are alive?"

"I found out what interests them, and I talk to them on that subject," Catherine answered.

"And what is that subject?"

"God," Catherine said. "God fascinates them, poor things. They don't know anything about Him!"

In the middle of another dinner in London, Catherine was handed a cable from New York.

"Must sign Boris Bulgaria. Thirty thousand limit. Get busy."

A rival agency had induced Queen Marie of Roumania to make a lecture tour in the United States. Emmerich, therefore, was determined to counter with the King of Bulgaria; and Catherine felt she must not fail.

She made her excuses, taxied to her hotel, packed, and sped to Sophia.

As she walked through the principal square of the city she saw a monument erected in honor of those who had fought for the liberation of Bulgaria from the Turks. She looked for her father's name and found it. She went to see the prime minister with confidence.

"I am delighted to meet the daughter of Colonel de Kolyschkine," the prime minister said. "He was wounded in our country's cause. We owe him and his a debt we can never pay. I await your command, Baroness."

Catherine went into the matter obliquely, and found the minister more than willing to listen.

"This is a supreme opportunity for His Majesty to replenish his personal fortunes," she said, "as well as to interest the United States in the problems, the resources, and the friendship of Bulgaria. Who can say what new industries may be financed here because of His Majesty's conversation with American capitalists? Or who can say that some beautiful and rich American woman . . ."

The minister smiled and held up a warning hand; then said discreetly that the king, no matter how many beautiful and wealthy ladies he might meet in America, would never forget the daughter of the House of Savoy.

"There is something there," he said, "that — well, His Majesty burns with hope for the Italian princess."

"May I see His Majesty," Catherine asked, "and talk business to him?"

"You may talk to him confidentially, and at length," the minister promised, and gave her all the credentials she needed.

Catherine hurried to the palace, a shabby building, but the King was not there. She discovered him in the garage, lying underneath a somewhat battered automobile, and tinkering with its vitals.

He rolled himself out when Catherine spoke, wiped his grease-stained hands on some cotton waste, brushed his dusty overalls, and made his visitor welcome.

He liked the idea of the American trip, but not too much.

"Thirty thousand dollars," he said. "That is an enormous amount of money. I could paint the palace with that. And buy new uniforms for the palace guard. I could — but America is so far away! And there is a girl in Italy. . . ."

"A beautiful princess."

"Ah yes," the King sighed. "How beautiful she is!"

"And you will need money for her, if you marry, Your Majesty."

The king asked for a few days to think it over; and asked Catherine to return for her answer on the second day.

Catherine taxied to her hotel and cabled New York that the king was young and handsome — and already in the bag. Then she started to her room. The hotel clerk intercepted her before she reached the elevator. He bowed very low and asked if he might have a word with the "American baroness."

He looked furtively around to be sure no one was close

enough to overhear what he was going to say, then whispered:

"There is a Russian who insists that he must see you, Baroness. But he is so ragged I felt you could not be annoyed with him. I bade him wait outside the lobby, where he would not be seen. If the baroness would like to meet him there —"

"Of course," Catherine said. "Bring me to the man."

Tears smarted her eyes as she looked upon the ragged visitor. He was unbelievably thin. But he was as tall and straight as ever. He was as imperious and as handsome.

"Nick!" she cried.

"Katia! It is really you?"

For this man's soul, Catherine had had a hundred Masses said. It wasn't easy to grasp the fact that he was not dead.

She said his name, as though saying it would make the fact of his being alive more evident. "Nicholas Makletzoff."

And then a thousand questions clamored at her lips for utterance. "What happened? Where have you been? Why did you never write to us?" But she did not utter a single question.

"Wait," she said. "We can talk later. We're going to have the finest dinner anybody ever ate in Sophia, with all the caviar there is in Bulgaria, and all the champagne and vodka you can drink. But first we are going shopping."

Nicholas looked down at his clothes. They were clean and well brushed, but they would never do for any formal occasion.

"Katia, it must be true," he said. "They told me you were a fabulously rich American noblewoman. But I cannot accept —"

"Nonsense." Catherine cut him short. "I have a fabulous expense account, and you can owe me what I spend on your wardrobe. I've been staying at mother's, so my expenses haven't been as high as they might have been. Here's where I catch up."

Nicholas didn't know what she meant by expense accounts. He had understood only that her mother was still alive.

"Tell me about her," he demanded. "She is well? And your father, and your brothers, and your husband?"

"Mother and Serge and Andrew are in Belgium. You'll meet the whole family as soon as I've finished my business with the King."

Nicholas was bothered again.

"The King? I don't understand. You mean the King of Bulgaria? Katia, don't talk nonsense."

"Of course the King of Bulgaria. I just left him. He's quite a man."

"Katia, do not torment me. You cannot talk to the King of Bulgaria. You cannot even get close to him."

They went shopping, and they went to dinner, and the story of years was related in a few minutes.

Nick was a cousin of Catherine and Boris de Hueck. He had served with Boris in the engineers. After the revolution, he had joined Wrangle's army. When Catherine last heard of him he was in the retreat to Odessa.

He was the engineer of the locomotive on the last train in the retreat, he told her, and was one of the few to escape slaughter by the Reds.

When they arrived at Odessa they met a French force, and were taken to Gallipoli.

"We were left there on the beach," Nicholas said. "I was so crippled with rheumatic fever I could not move a muscle. My body was as stiff as a board. There weren't any doctors around, as you might imagine. We lived in rough barracks. We helped each other. Every morning my comrades carried me to the sea shore, stripped me, and left me to lie all day in the sun and the sand. At night they brought me back to our barracks."

After three months of this treatment, Nicholas began to move his arms and legs. After six months he was comparatively well. He had no money, of course. Nobody had. He sought work, as his friends did, in Bulgaria or Roumania or Constantinople. He was lucky enough, he said, to get a job on a railroad in Bulgaria. He spent most of the day naked from the waist up, and soon gained back all his old strength.

When the Bulgarians learned he had been an architect and engineer, they put him in charge of a gang of men building a bridge. That was his occupation when somebody told him about the rich Baroness de Hueck who was stopping at the hotel in Sophia. He had received but a few cents a day for his labors, and had subsisted on bread, cheese made from the milk of sheep, and "cold, clear water."

"It would take me years, at my pay," he said, "to save enough to buy a dinner such as this."

"Don't worry about that," Catherine said. "It doesn't cost me anything. The lecture bureau in New York is buying it. Wait until I've got you established in Canada, and you can buy me a dinner better than this."

"Canada? Katia, are you mad? How can I get to Canada?"

"Don't worry about it now. I'll fix it. An American woman can do anything. I'll see the prime minister tomorrow and fix up your papers. If I have to, I'll see the King himself about you. I'll get you to Toronto. There's a Russian colony there. You can find a job there, with your talents. You can teach my son, George, to speak Russian."

Nicholas shook his head.

"How many times I dreamed you were dead," he said. "And now you throw away money like it was nothing, you talk about the King as if he were a friend of yours, you speak of taking me to Canada as if it were nothing at all — and maybe I am only dreaming you are here, talking to me. I am confused. I feel I shall wake up with the hot sun on my naked back and a shovel in my hand. Katia, are you real?"

A bellboy came into the dining room with a cable from New York.

"Marie a flop. Cancel king."

"We'll be leaving for Brussels in a day or two," Catherine said. "I've got to cancel King Boris — and don't tell me I can't do it. What about a dinner for some of your friends before we go? A sort of farewell banquet?"

"Impossible," Nicholas said. "I have at least twenty good friends; and nobody could — "

"Bring them all," Catherine commanded. "I'll hire an orchestra. I'll select the wines. I'll go into a conference with the chef and select a menu of Russian dishes. Want to help me?"

It was a great banquet. It was a memorable night not only for the Russian refugees, the hungry and hard-working men who must remain in exile for the rest of their lives, but for Catherine as well.

The bill reached the staggering sum of ten dollars in American money!

The next morning they left for Brussels.

"The day before we left for New York," Catherine says, "I picked up the Bible mother used to read to us so often in the evening at Antrea. She was showing it to Nick, with other things she had managed to bring from Antrea. A few withered flowers fell out of it. The tops of daisies. Flowers without stems. Petals stained and yellowed and crumpled.

" 'Why on earth are you saving these things?' I asked.

" 'You gave them to me years ago,' Mother answered. "We were walking through a field of daisies and you snatched up these flowers and handed them to me, all dirty and torn and mussed. I was so touched I cried. And I've saved them ever since.'

"That was like the rosary, I thought. With our sinful hands we pluck a bouquet of Hail Mary's for our blessed Mother. We are sleepy or tired, and usually inattentive, when we offer these flowers to her. But don't you realize she treasures them in her heart, and that she wants to show them to us again, some day?"

≫ 17 ≪

FOR approximately two years after the talent-scout trip abroad, Catherine managed foreign celebrities in America, and sometimes went on tour with them, and with such American authors as Heywood Broun, William Seabrook, Sherwood Anderson, Countee Cullen, and Floyd Dell. She also acted as literary agent for a number of English and French authors.

Now and then she had to travel all over the country to make sure her lecturers had every comfort. They were so helpless! Count Herman Keyserling was one who depended on her for nearly everything.

The count, after the publication of his *Diary of a Philosopher*, became extremely popular in the United States. He was unpopular only with the hosts and hostesses who opened their homes to him.

He was a big man, and complained bitterly of the lack of space in Pullman berths. Catherine had to register these complaints in every city he visited. He had to have oysters every day, whether they were in season or not; and it was Catherine's job to see that his host provided them. He had to have champagnes and white wines every day, in spite of Prohibition. Catherine didn't have to supply these vintages, but it was her duty to acquaint Keyserling's hosts with his desires.

She had acquired stocks and bonds, a nice income, a beautiful flat on Fifth Avenue, a car, an extensive wardrobe, and a country residence — a farmhouse at Graymoor, near Peekskill, on the Hudson. And for the first time in her busy life, she was able to keep her son George close to her.

It was not by accident that she acquired the house at Graymoor. She wanted to be close to the monks and nuns who made Graymoor their home. She loved Father Paul, who organized the Society of the Atonement and built the monastery there. And she loved Mother Lurana who was in charge of the convent.

In those weird days when she was looking for work in the big city, and starving, she had gone to the Jesuits on 16th Street, and fainted before the door was opened. Someone carried her inside and revived her. And a smiling priest saw that she had a well-cooked steak to eat.

"Why don't you go up to Graymoor for a rest?" he asked. "You will have a cozy room there, good food and plenty of it, leisure, advice, fresh air, and everything else you need. You'll be a new woman in a week."

Catherine told him about the convent door that had been closed against her poverty and hunger.

"You will find real charity at Graymoor," the priest assured her. "Both Father Paul and Mother Lurana are living saints. They will take excellent care of you, asking no questions, seeking no money. They will see Christ in you. They see Him in every man or woman who comes to them in need."

Catherine had never heard of Graymoor or of Father Paul or of Mother Lurana. The priest told her something of their history.

"They were Anglicans. When they became Catholics they opened the doors of the monastery and the convent to all who might come. Everybody is welcome. Many have gone to them, and some have stayed to become priests or lay brothers or nuns — or just to help as they may.

"Father Paul is one of the best-known characters in New York. You can see him often in the city, in his brown Franciscan habit, with the crucifix against his heart. He may be standing in front of a subway stile, waiting to beg a nickel from someone. He never has any money because he gives it away to the unfortunate. Or you may see him in Grand Central, waiting for somebody to buy him a ticket to Graymoor."

Catherine had gone to Graymoor; and she had been there only a little time when she became a Franciscan tertiary, and a part-time secretary to Mother Lurana.

"I saw a miracle while I was there," she declares. "I came into the chapel one morning, early, just as Father Paul was rising from his knees. He used to spend hours kneeling before the Blessed Sacrament. This particular morning there was a woman and a little girl waiting for him. The girl had a withered hand, and the mother had asked Father Paul to pray for her.

"Father Paul walked toward the two, put his hand over the little girl's hand, and held it for many seconds. When he removed his hand, the child wriggled her fingers. Her hand was completely cured. I fainted. When I came to, Father Paul was beckoning to me. 'Don't tell anybody about this,' he bade me, 'until after I am dead.'

"Mother Lurana, who died many years before Father Paul's death, has already been made a Venerable by Rome; and I am sure that someday both she and the priest will be canonized, and will be as revered by Catholics all over the world as are St. Francis and St. Clare."

Before Catherine left Graymoor — to return to New York and the constant battle with jobs and hunger — she promised herself that someday she would buy a house near the convent and live there with George as long as she could.

Now, as general office manager for Emmerich and Lee, she commuted by auto, between the farmhouse and the flat on Fifth Avenue. While she was at work, a governess took care of the boy.

He was about six the day he went out into the fields alone and ate some poisonous berries. The governess called a doctor and notified Catherine. Catherine drove home at seventy miles an hour.

"The boy is deathly sick," the doctor told her. "He must have an operation within three hours to remove an obstruction to the bowels or I cannot be accountable for him."

Father Paul had come into the house as the doctor talked. He arranged for an immediate operation in the Presbyterian hospital in New York. "You have plenty of time to get there," he said, as he carried George to the car. "Don't worry. Have faith. Everything will be all right."

Catherine had faith, but it wavered. She drove madly. She went around sharp curves without slowing. A motorcycle policeman gave chase and overtook her. But when she explained her errand, he went ahead of her car, siren blowing to clear a path even in the traffic of New York.

While the boy was being wheeled into the operating room he recovered, seemingly through a miracle. He sat up on the stretcher, smiling at his mother, and demanding something to eat.

Before Catherine could say anything to him a nurse hurried up.

"There is a telephone message for you," she said. "Long distance."

It was Father Paul on the other end of the line.

"You're coming back now that George is all right?" he asked.

"Yes, Father; but how did you know?"

"I knew," he said. "God bless you. And don't drive so fast."

Through Mother Lurana, Catherine learned that as soon as her car had left the farm Father Paul strode into the chapel and prostrated himself before the altar. He remained there more than hour, his arms outstretched. Then he arose and told Mother Lurana that George no longer needed an operation.

Anybody who knew the Baroness Catherine de Hueck at the height of her career would have said she was a success. For sometime Catherine herself was of that opinion.

But the life she saw at Graymoor, the simplicity, the holiness, the abundant charity, the unworldliness, and the miraculous events that came to her attention, led her to regard herself as a colossal failure.

She knelt in a pew at St. Pat's and bent her head in prayer.

"Lord," she said, "I am a rich woman and growing richer and more ambitious every day. I am concerned about myself, my job, my money, my stocks and bonds, my furniture, my future.

"Was it for this You protected me through wars and revolutions? Was it for this You taught me the terrible needs of the poor? Was it for this I sang the *Magnificat* in the days of my starvation — that I should become rich and forget Your little ones?

"Behold the city swarms with the poor. They are all about me. They multiply every day. But I do nothing. And I grow richer. I want to help, but my son is still young, and my mother and my brothers still need me. What shall I do?"

She seemed to hear a voice:

"My grace is sufficient for all. Can you not trust Me, even as a little child trusts her father?"

She had no answer.

She prayed again. "I love good clothes, good things to eat, a good car to drive. Must I give them up? I love books, music, travel. Must I give them up, too? How can I help Your poor if I myself am poor?"

And again she seemed to hear a voice:

"Oh you of little faith!"

She went back to the office and resigned. She sold the car, the furniture of the New York apartment, and most everything she had in the farmhouse. She saved enough money for George's schooling, and her own immediate needs, and gave the rest to the poor.

She had no definite plans, only a hazy idea of becoming a working girl again, for the benefit of her soul. She decided to return to Canada. And, for reasons she couldn't quite define, chose Montreal instead of Toronto as the place to begin her "reformation."

She had loved Montreal. She had been happy there whenever her lectures took her to that city. And she thought it would be well to place George in the school of the French Christian Brothers. There was no school like it in Toronto.

She got a job in the book department of the T. Eaton store in Montreal and rented a house on Hope Avenue. When she was settled she took her son to the school.

A venerable old lay brother greeted the two in the corridor, speaking in French.

"This child does not belong here," he said. "He belongs to the Jesuits of D'Autremont. Take him there, and God bless you both."

"Thank you," Catherine said, and turned away.

She didn't find anything strange in this odd encounter until days later, after George had been accepted by the Jesuits. Then she began to wonder at the venerable man, and what he had said to her. He hadn't talked to George. He had scarcely looked at him. What made him say George didn't belong there?

But after she learned that he was Brother Andre — another candidate for canonization — she ceased to wonder.

Her hazy idea about helping God's poor began to clarify as she worked in the big department store. She became convinced that she must dedicate herself to a life of poverty and service, and that ridiculous as it seemed, she could best help the poor by being one of them.

She began to realize that God had taught her this lesson by letting her be poor and helpless, and by letting organized charities snub and deny her. Organized charities had money and influence and great power. They were not of the poor, but for the poor. They did not feel for the poor as individuals, but as "cases."

"God has shaped me to work with and for the poor, as one of them," she thought. "It is nearly time for me to do His will. But first I must know more than I do now about nursing the sick and the injured. And I must know more, much more, about psychology and theology, that I may nurse minds and souls as well as bodies."

She quit the book department. She left the house. She went to work in the Montreal General Hospital. And she took a course in moral theology.

When she returned to Toronto, in 1930, she had a clear idea of her vocation. But before she could put it into practice, Archbishop Neil McNeil asked her to make an investigation for him.

"In the past few years," he said, "approximately 28,000 Catholics of the 96,000 in this archdiocese have left the Church and joined the Communist party. I want you to find out why."

For months Catherine frequented Communist circles. She was well received, for she looked poor, and was given all the information she sought. She was regarded as a "Comrade," a "fellow traveler," even by many of her friends. They criticized her severely, but she did not let them know they were unjust.

Every week she made reports to the Archbishop, keeping him thoroughly informed on the work of the Communists, their intentions, and the plans they were making to extend their work.

When she had finished her investigation she wrote a ninety-six page report and presented it to His Excellency, waiting while he leafed through it.

"I pointed out," she says, "that Communists are made by the hypocrisy of Christians who are Christians only in name. One indifferent Christian may breed a dozen fervent Communists.

"In times of stress, in panic or depression, in layoff or strike, the poor cry out for help. Few Catholics ever heed those cries or help in any way. But the atheistic Communists come forward, arms laden with groceries. Or they ride to the rescue on trucks filled with coal.

"Communists make converts of the poor because they are poor themselves and sincere in their irreligion. We Catholics could convert all the Communists on earth, if we were really Catholics and obeyed the commandments of Christ as truly as the Communists obey the commands of Moscow. There wouldn't be any Communists, if we were really Catholics."

The Archbishop looked troubled after he had glanced through the long report.

"What would you do if you were I?" he asked.

"I do not know," she said. "I am not an archbishop. But I know what I must do. I must live in voluntary poverty, in the slums. I must beg bread for myself, for those who may join me, and for the poor around me. I must work with and for the poor, and aid them in every way I can. Only one thing makes me hesitate. I have a son, now nine years old."

The prelate pondered his reply, fingering the pectoral cross that hung from a chain around his neck.

"The lay apostolate!" he said. "That requires a special vocation, Catherine."

"I know that, Your Excellency."

"To leave the world, and yet not leave it. To beggar yourself that you may enrich others. To have nothing and give everything. This is the most noble ideal any Christian can set up for himself. But I want you to think it over for a year, in prayer and meditation, and then come back to me."

At this time Catherine lived in a house on Isabella Street, and maintained herself and her son by renting rooms.

"I organized a study club in that house," she said, "with a number of other women as crazy as myself. We called our little group 'The Guild of Our Lady of the Atonement.' No doubt you can see the Graymoor influence in that title."

At the end of the year she returned to the Archbishop with George.

"Are you still of the same mind?" the prelate asked.

"I am even more convinced than I was a year ago that I have a vocation to the lay apostolate," Catherine answered.

The Archbishop talked to George.

"Son," he said. "You are ten years old now. You have long since reached the age of reason. You can go voluntarily with your mother into this new life, or you can refuse to go. But I must know first that you realize all that such a life entails."

George was silent.

"It means that your mother must give up all she has, move

into some frightful place in the slums, sleep in a room likely to be infested with bedbugs, roaches, and vermin of all sorts, and become a beggar for herself and her associates and all those she hopes to feed, comfort, teach, clothe, or nurse."

"You mean my mother wants to try to be a saint?"

The Bishop laughed gently, and said, "Perhaps."

"Well" — George looked quite serious — "whatever she does, I want to be with her."

The saintly old man closed his eyes for a moment, and bent his head.

"Then you shall go with her," he said. "But you must have a room of your own. A clean room. You must have special food, such as a growing boy needs. You must have decent clothes. And you must have decent schooling."

"These things," Catherine said, "he will have."

They knelt, and the Archbishop blessed them.

⋙ 18 ⋘

THE first Friendship House opened its door on October 15, 1931, the feast of St. Teresa of Ávila, in a tumble-down, red-brick house at 128 Portland Street, in the slums of Toronto.

It encountered hostility and suspicion. Catherine, and the girls who volunteered to work with her, were ridiculed, spat upon, even stoned. Yet they went to Mass and Communion every morning, walking through the wretchedest streets in the city, gladly exposing themselves to insult and injury.

Gradually women began to speak to them furtively. "Pray for me." And gradually they began to go to the crazy little house for food, for clothes, for help in dire need, for sympathy and advice — and even for some knowledge of religion.

Soon there was a Friendship House in Hamilton, and another in Ottawa. They were teaching children, nursing the sick, clothing the ragged, feeding the poor of the neighborhood and the homeless men who came in uncounted thousands off the freight trains, and spreading the Word in ever widening circles.

Some Communist centers closed, some poor families began to take hope and to thrive, seven "hobos" decided to become Catholic priests, and other wonders occurred.

But the need for lay apostles was most pressing in New York City's Harlem, and the baroness was invited to come with her staff workers and make this her field.

She had been in Harlem more than three years before Mr. Dee first saw her; and there were five store fronts to keep her busy, many staff workers, and scores of volunteers. Each of those store fronts had been converted into a unit of Friendship House. There was a library, a room where clothing was dispensed to all who asked for it, and recreation and study rooms for the children. Also there was a flat where the staff workers and the visitors sat down to a meal cooked by the baroness — and where some of the staff workers slept, after a long, hard day.

The meals were never pretentious. Sometimes there was nothing to eat but cornflakes — with water, there being no milk available. Frequently it was soup. Once in a while there was only tea and toast, and no butter for the toast. Occasionally somebody donated a ham or a turkey or a dozen or two thick steaks. But no matter what was brought to the table everyone ate with relish, Negroes and whites. There was more fun at the table than anywhere else in New York. After dinner they prayed together, staff workers and visitors, saying Compline as equal children of God.

Mr. Dee was fascinated by the life of Friendship House, by the philosophy of the foundress and of the "kids" who worked with her, and by the open forums held every Monday night. Then the library was packed with people of different colors and creeds and conditions in life; and a speaker might talk on Negro housing, juvenile delinquency, divorce, the Mass, or some other vital topic.

He was amazed at the constant mention of the Holy Ghost, and the incessant reiteration of the phrase, "to do the will of God." He had never seen boys and girls like these, nor heard them talk so openly of God. The average Catholic, he was shocked to discover, was ashamed or afraid to talk publicly of his religion or his God. These people loved to talk of nothing else.

Ever since he had been old enough to listen, he reflected, people had used the phrase, "the will of God," to signify that someone had died or gone crazy, to cloak a failure, to excuse a crime, or to explain a calamity such as a crop failure, a famine, a flood, a conflagration, or a war.

Here the phrase was used to explain the ordinary routine of the day.

The baroness gave him a book to read, *Brebeuf and His Brethren*, by the Canadian poet, E. J. Pratt, and pointed out these lines:

> This is the end of man — *Deum laudet* —
> To seek and find the will of God, to act
> Upon it for the ordering of life,
> And for the soul's beatitude. . . .

"How can anyone be happy," she demanded, "who does not seek and find the will of God, and subject himself to it?"

But this is not the story of Friendship House. Catherine has written about the work in Toronto and Hamilton and Ottawa and New York and Chicago and Marathon, Wis., in her book *Friendship House*.

And she has mentioned "the little village of Combermere, in Ontario, lying sleepily by the shores of the Madawaska river . . . a silvery trail of breath-taking beauty."

It was in an unpretentious East Side restaurant — she hated the expensive, the crowded, the garish, and the vulgar dining rooms of New York — that she first talked of Combermere to Mr. Dee.

She had stopped in the middle of a story about her childhood in Egypt.

"It is the most beautiful place on earth," she said.

"Egypt?"

"Of course not."

She seemed surprised at such an idiotic remark.

"Explain it, then," Mr. Dee pleaded. "You were a child in Egypt, and it is the most beautiful place on earth — only of course it isn't."

She was amused. "Gosh! I got to thinking how different Egypt is from Russia. Naturally that made me think of Canada, which is like Russia in many ways, especially in winter. And that brought my thoughts to Combermere."

"And what is Combermere?"

"A tiny village about 130 miles west of Ottawa. A friend of mine, a woman doctor in Vermont, sends me money enough to go there every year for a rest. She insists I travel by Pullman. So I do."

"Do you fish?"

"Oh yes. I love fishing. The river's full of bass, pike, pickerel, catfish, and other varieties. But it isn't the fishing itself that means so much to me. It's being out in the open, on the water, in the sun and the wind, or in the shade of some great tree that towers over the bank. It's watching the changing light. It's meditating. Sometimes the Son of Man seems to come walking over the water toward the boat. Sometimes, at sundown, He splashes the hills and the skies and the stream with glowing colors. Sometimes He pins the moon and the stars on the river's surface.

"Mr. Dee, it's like being in heaven for a time."

"And you come joyfully back to the hell of Harlem! Don't you ever think of quitting all this and living in Combermere?"

The question disquieted and horrified her.

"How could I leave Friendship House? God put me here. I expect to stay here the rest of my life. I'm married to Friendship House, to the work of the lay apostolate. I am thankful for one month in the year in Canada."

"Pine trees, I suppose," Mr. Dee said. "And sandy roads. A blue river. Mountains. Lakes all around. A little shack . . ."

"It's not a shack. Nicholas is building a beautiful house there. Nicholas Makletzoff. I told you about him. He's an architect and an engineer; but he's also a painter — an artist — a musician, a carpenter — and a great fisherman. He planned the house, mapping a place for every joist, every floor board, every brick in the fireplace. And he is superintending the building."

"Yet you spend your life in the dirt and stench and sweat and miseries of Harlem."

"It is never easy to follow Christ," she explained softly. "Once in Toronto I thought it was too hard. I was young and strong, then, and I worked much harder than I do now. But I thought I couldn't stand it.

"I went to Archbishop McNeil, and told him I was through.

" 'Catherine,' he said, 'do you mind taking that crucifix off the wall and giving it to me?'

"I thought he hadn't heard a word I said, that he was just a sweet old saint wrapped up in some holy meditation. I got the crucifix, dusted it off, and handed it to him.

" 'Who is crucified here?' he asked.

" 'Our Redeemer,' I said.

"He bowed his head and turned the crucifix in his hand. 'And what is this empty space for?' he asked. 'Who is to be crucified there?'

"I answered almost without thinking. 'Anyone who loves Him. I, myself — if I may.' "

Mr. Dee felt stepped on.

"You won't quit, of course. But — "

"You think I'm making a sacrifice?" She shook her head earnestly from side to side, the light winking on her blue earrings. "Once I thought I had given up everything for Him. My books, my love of travel, my friends in New York, my people across the sea. I thought I should live and die in the slums, and be buried in some potter's field, where so many of God's poor find rest. And what did I get in return?

"There are more books in Friendship House than I can read. I have never traveled so much. I have a hundred times as many friends, and they are all over North America. And I have seen my people several times since then. I went to Europe twice, as a correspondent for the *Sign*, the Catholic monthly. I even had adventures in the Spanish Civil War and in World War II. I was in Warsaw when the blitz began. I walked over the Carpathian mountains to get away. God saved my life a dozen times on that trip. And — and I know that He is looking after my mother and my brothers over there now."

She had heard from her brother, Serge. He had married an English girl, and he was serving in the British army. Andrew, married to a Spanish woman, was in a concentration camp. Her mother, in her seventies, still lived in Brussels — but there was no news of her.

It was not until years later that she learned all her relatives had come safely through the war. Andrew had escaped from a concentration camp, changed his name, found work, had been placed in a second camp, and had escaped again. Before the war ended he had been given a sizable factory by the man who sheltered him from the Nazis.

Mme. Kolyschkine had managed to eke out the scanty food rations — and to feed some of her neighbors. Ever since she took the house in Brussels she had saved everything that might someday come in handy. String. Wrapping paper. Newspapers. Nails. Screws. Candles. The Russian revolution had taught her the value of these things.

During the German occupation there was a shortage of materials. Catherine's mother could get a little butter for a few sheets of wrapping paper and a hundred feet of twine. Her newspapers, which could also be used as wrapping paper, were traded for other foodstuffs. The nails brought her an old coat. She had been able to get almost everything she needed — except a comfortable pair of shoes.

Serge had become an officer. And he was chosen as the official interpreter when the British army met the Red army near Berlin. He had come home unscathed.

Mr. Dee abruptly changed the subject, not only to disperse the mist that was gathering in her eyes, but also to reveal, in a roundabout sort of way, that he was going to leave New York.

"You've never met Bishop Sheil, the senior auxiliary bishop of Chicago, have you?"

"No. But I'd like to. He's done so much for America through his Catholic Youth Organization. We have that here. You know the Bishop?"

"Yes. I expect to see him soon. Maybe someday — "

He left the sentence unfinished. "But you were talking about Egypt."

Mr. Dee was a widower. His first wife, Marie, had died in the influenza epidemic in Chicago, in 1918. His second wife, Mildred, had been killed in an accident in Beverly Hills, California, in 1939.

He lived in Larchmont, N. Y., with his younger son, Jack, and a housekeeper, Mrs. Julia Kusterer. His older boy, Eddie Jr., was married and the father of two sons.

Mr. Dee had worked for many years as a staff writer for a national weekly, but the magazine had been sold, and he had determined to go back into newspaper work. There was a paper starting in Chicago, his home town, and he had managed to get a job in its editorial department.

He wouldn't see much of Catherine. Maybe it was all for the best. She was too much in love with God to bother about any man. She was too wrapped up in Friendship House, even if she did fall in love with somebody. An incomparable woman, but also an unattainable woman. Yes, maybe it was all for the best. Maybe it was the will of God.

It wasn't until the day he left New York that he told her the news. He told it over the phone.

She didn't understand at first.

"You mean you are going to live in Chicago? Permanently?"

"From now on," he said.

"And — and we won't see you any more at Friendship House?"

Mr. Dee tried to say something, but couldn't.

"Oh Eddie, my heart is broken."

Mr. Dee said good-by, hurriedly. The man was waiting to disconnect the phone. The house was empty and clean. Bare walls. Bare floors. It had looked like that when he and Mildred first saw it, years before.

But the book of Mildred was closed.

And so, Mr. Dee thought, was the book of Catherine.

He closed the door softly behind him, got into his car, and started on the long road to Chicago, followed by the van that held his furniture.

There was an empty house behind him, and, he felt, an empty life ahead. Yet he was not altogether unhappy.

For the first time since he had known her, Catherine had

called him by his first name. And there had been something in her voice that reminded him of Mildred, and of Marie before her.

"Oh Eddie, my heart is broken!"

She didn't mean that, of course. It was just a way of saying, "Good-by, God bless you." And yet —

He had been in Chicago only a few weeks when she sent him a wire. She was flying in from St. Louis. She had a series of lectures to deliver in and around Chicago. Would Mr. Dee meet her at the airport?

He was there an hour ahead of time. He watched the plane land, saw her poised on the top step of the landing platform, looking for him. She looked thin and haggard and ill — and joyous. He wanted to run to greet her. But he didn't.

"Hello," he said. "Welcome to the city. You have a date to meet His Excellency, the Most Reverend Bernard J. Sheil, who thinks you are pretty swell — and you have a date with me for breakfast, lunch, and dinner, every day you're here. We have a house in Wilmette. Twenty rooms. You could drill a regiment in some of them. But it's a home. And there's a room for you. Mrs. K has everything ready for you."

They met the Bishop the next day.

"Baroness," he said, "what does one do to get a Friendship House in Chicago?"

"One simply asks, Your Excellency," Catherine replied.

"Then I'm asking you now. I shall see Archbishop Stritch, naturally, but I am sure he will welcome you and your staff workers to Chicago as gladly as I do. How much money will you need?"

"Whatever the Holy Ghost will send."

The Bishop laughed.

"Naturally, but how much do you want from me?"

It was Catherine who laughed then.

"Not a penny," she said. "Friendship House has no endowment. No man or woman underwrites its expenses, or gives it any sort of subsidy. We beg for money when we need it — and it always comes, though sometimes we pray harder than usual before we get it. For a long time we depended on my lectures."

"But I insist — for one year, anyway — on helping you along. Say, then, a thousand dollars?"

Catherine was beaten before she began to fight. "The voice of the Bishop," she said, "is always the voice of God."

On a gray morning in November Mr. Dee suggested a ride out into the country north and west of Chicago.

Catherine put on a blue hat and a blue veil.

"You remember this?" she asked.

"Yes. You wore it the last time I saw you in New York. It came out of your clothing room. You are very beautiful, Catherine. And the hat has nothing to do with it. Nor the veil."

They stopped at a wayside inn and ordered sandwiches. Mr. Dee put a nickel in the juke box, and Catherine hummed a few words of the tune it played.

"I don't want to set the world afire."

Something in Mr. Dee's gaze made her look serious, and deepened the blue of her eyes.

"A penny for your thoughts, Mr. Dee."

He had been thinking that she was free. Only a few weeks ago he had learned she was no longer married to the Baron. She had been granted an annulment after years of investigation by Church authorities. On what grounds she had sought that annulment, on what grounds the decree had been granted, he did not know, did not care to know.

"A penny?" he said. "These are dollar thoughts."

She was free, he was thinking, yet she wasn't free at all. She never would be free! She was bound more tightly to Friendship House than she could ever be bound to any husband. It would be madness to make love to her. A man could get badly hurt that way.

But what did that matter, after all?

"I was thinking of you," he told her. "It's always been you."

He saw the light drain out of her eyes, watched the color wash out of her cheeks then surge back in a crimson tide, noticed the trembling of her wide lips, heard a quick indrawn breath, and felt alarmed as she rose from the table and hurried out of the inn.

She had not said a word.

Mr. Dee kept his chair for a moment, not sure of what had happened. The music was still playing.

"I just want to start

A flame in your heart. . . ."

He placed some money carefully near his glass and went out slowly.

She was in the car, her face hidden in her hands. She moved away from him, across the red leather cushion. He seated himself behind the wheel. For a moment he thought of starting the car and driving away, fast. Instead he moved close to her. He put his arms about her, and told her not to be afraid.

They drove home without another word between them. And late that night they sat before a fireplace, staring at the flames, listening to the hiss and crackle of the burning logs.

"So it's come at last," Catherine broke the silence. "I never expected it. Not from you, at least. If I had known how you felt, I would have sent you away long ago. And if I had suspected myself — but I didn't. I hadn't the least suspicion.

"What are we going to do?" Mr. Dee asked.

"What can we do? There is a barrier between us we cannot get over, under, nor around. Do you know now why I ran?"

Mr. Dee shook his head to indicate he knew.

"You think I was afraid of love?"

"Yes."

"You are wrong, Mr. Dee. I ran from the cross."

"It is a crucifixion, isn't it?"

"To be my age and to discover love — after the arid, empty years — and to realize one must give it up. . . . Never did a cross seem so hard to me, nor so cruel."

"You never loved the Baron?"

"I was a child when I married him, an immature girl still playing with her dolls. I never loved any man, until now. And now it is too late."

Mr. Dee found courage somewhere.

"Well, let's not be tragic about it, Catherine."

"One makes a supreme sacrifice to God," she answered, "not with tears, but with a joyous heart. It is good to have so great a gift to offer. What have I ever given Him half so precious, half so dear to me?"

"Someday," said Mr. Dee, "the barrier may vanish. Anyway, I'm going to keep on asking you to marry me."

"Please do," she whispered, "though I keep saying 'no.' "

❧ 19 ❧

ON THE evening of December 3, 1941, a few minutes after the last final edition of the *Chicago Daily News* had hit the pavement — and but a few days before the first Japanese bombs hit Pearl Harbor — great presses began to labor. And, shortly afterward, a litter of 900,000 copies of the new paper, Marshall Field's *Chicago Sun,* was given to a waiting world.

There was no pealing of joyful bells. There was no dancing in the streets. There were no brass bands to welcome the newcomer. But there was a celebration in all the offices of the paper. And in the tower of the building, Mr. Field entertained a host of friends.

Catherine accompanied Mr. Dee into the plant that night. The guards at the elevator, stationed there to keep the sheep from the goats, bowed low to her. Reporters, editors, copy boys, and columnists welcomed her — and later described her as "the lady with the accent and the veil." And Mr. Dee showed her through "the works."

At 4 o'clock in the morning he suggested they take the first edition of the paper to the house in Logan Square where his family resided.

"You're crazy," Catherine objected. "You want to wake up your mother and everybody else? They'll murder you. And they should."

"You've got a lot to learn, Russian," Mr. Dee said. "They'll get out of bed with three rousing *vivas* and a Bronx cheer, and give us bacon and eggs."

In the taxi, summoned by Mr. Dee's magic wand, Catherine protested vehemently. Mr. Dee silenced her with a lengthy explanation.

"The house on Sawyer Avenue is a sort of Grand Hotel where everything happens, and is supposed to. Let me tell you about the gang. I have two sisters. Kathleen is a court reporter, with her own office. Eileen is a school teacher. Mother's seventy-something, and the boss of the house. The rest of us are newspapermen. All but the black sheep, that is.

"Jim is on the *Tribune* and the best reporter in the country. His specialties are politics and crime. He pretty nearly runs the town. He's broken down doors in the sheriff's office, and in the state's attorney's sanctum, and other places. He has had police captains shifted, has elected aldermen and judges and mayors. He does about as he pleases.

"He stands on the corner of LaSalle and Randolph every day at noon, and people come up and give him stories. He's been on the *Tribune* twenty-five years, and it's his bible. An army colonel once tried to bar him from entering an arsenal where a murder had been committed. He got mad at the things Jim said. 'What do you think the army is?' he thundered. He didn't get any further. Not with Jim. 'And what do you think the *Chicago Tribune* is,' Jim shouted, 'and where do you think you are? West Point? Get out of my way or I'll walk over you.'"

"So he went to jail," Catherine guessed.

"Hey," Mr. Dee reproved her. "This is Chicago. He went into the armory. The colonel followed him — meekly — with all the other newspapermen."

"Go on," she said.

"Bill is a swell reporter too. He's on the *Times*. He also breaks down doors. But the cops say he doesn't break them as politely as Jim does. He's twenty years younger than I am. He's married to a beautiful black-haired girl, whose name was Marjorie O'Malley.

"Frank's on the *Sun,* and going strong. He and his wife, Mary, have a bunch of kids. Robert, the oldest, works in the *Tribune* reference room — the morgue. And Ray's going to work on the *Sun.*

"Tom, two years younger than Bill, is our Hearstling — a cub on the *Herald-American* — and he and Bill and Frank are the baseball nuts in the family. Bill and Tom have played catch with at least one cop who got in their way."

"You mean," she said, "they stopped their ball game to invite the officers to play with them?"

"No. Quite the contrary. Bill picked up a cop and threw him to Tom. Tom threw him back. The cop wouldn't play ball with them. So they played catch with him."

Catherine shook her head in wonder, not knowing whether to believe Mr. Dee or not, and not sure she understood him.

"And what about the black sheep — or is that something you'd rather not talk about?"

"Well, I suppose it's all right to tell you. It's Marty. He was on the *Tribune* once. He was a good reporter. He might have been a great reporter. But he gave it up. We don't usually discuss him."

"He went into trade, I suppose," said Catherine. "Is that the answer? And you newspaper aristocrats couldn't take it."

Mr. Dee shook his head.

"No," he whispered, "he became a priest. The Reverend Martin W. Doherty. But don't go shouting it all over Chicago."

She looked around for something to throw at him, then decided it was an American joke, and probably she should laugh.

The taxi stopped. Mr. Dee opened the front door of the house, turned on all the lights in the front rooms, and pulled the white and shaky baroness in.

"The *Sun* is out," he shouted. He crowed like a barnyard full of roosters. "Come on, get up and see the *Sun!*"

Echoes of the rooster call reassured Catherine.

Mother thrust her head out of her bedroom door.

"Welcome *Sun*," she said gaily. "Welcome, Son."

Kathleen and Eileen and Tom and Jim came out of their rooms, tousled, sleepy, cheerful, beaming at Mr. Dee and his bewildered friend; and presently coffee was being made, and platters of ham and eggs were being passed around the long table.

Jim looked at the *Sun* before breakfast was served and pretended to be violently ill.

"And you carried that rag all the way from the Loop?" he asked, looking aghast. "I'm glad it was dark, and nobody saw you."

"It's a free country," Tom broke in, apparently angry. "If a man wants to read a paper like this — well, that is his right, though maybe not his right mind. The *Sun* isn't so bad, but it does cry out for the freedom of suppression. Who's this punk, Doherty, that wrote the Sunbeam column? Some hick from New York?"

"If he's on the *Chicago Sun*," Jim said, "of course he's from out of town. What Chicago reporter would work for a sheet like that?"

Mr. Dee's mother turned to Catherine.

"Don't mind them," she said. "They won't kill one another. They always talk like that about their papers."

Mr. Dee noticed that Catherine ate very little. She was thinking of her own family, he decided, wondering how long a time it was since they had eaten a meal like this, how long before they would eat another — if they were still alive. And she was thinking of the millions of peasants in France and Germany and Italy and Russia who never had seen such abundance of well-cooked food so casually set on the table — and never would. She was thanking God for the blessings He had showered on America, and wondering why the people of America did not realize how fortunate they were.

"Yes," she acknowledged, in the taxi to Wilmette, "I was thinking all those things. And I was thinking how wonderful it would be if I could be part of your family. So big a family. But — 'the Lord giveth and the Lord taketh away, blessed be the name of the Lord.'"

She spread her fingers out before him.

"And you never noticed, Mr. Dee, that I polished my nails just for you. You like them?"

~≫ 20 ≪~

Mrs. Kusterer was bustling around the kitchen. Jack was trying to decide whether to get up or to sleep another hour. And Catherine sat with Mr. Dee over cold cups of coffee.

"God brought us together," she said softly. "God keeps us apart. His will be done."

"It reminds me of the Irishman," Mr. Dee said. "He was speaking about the mortar. 'Sure,' he says, 'it kapes the bricks apart, but it likewise kapes them togither.' We have made a common sacrifice. We can never really be far apart."

She picked up the little white and green coffeepot and caressed it — as though it were something warm to comfort her cold hands.

"All my life," she said, "I shall remember this coffeepot."

It was the last day of her stay in Chicago. Mr. Dee drove her to the train, and left her in the depot for a few minutes. He hurried to a florist shop and bought several dozens of roses. Long stemmed. Blood red. Fragrant. Beautiful enough for an empress. He kissed her good-by, and put the flowers in her arms.

"I kept your roses fresh with my tears all the way to New York," she wrote. "I placed them over my heart, and felt the thorns in my flesh. I never want to see red roses again."

The days were gray in Chicago. Mr. Dee was sent all over America by the *Sun*. He was given big stories to cover, or he was allowed to sit in the office and read magazines or books

— or to do whatever else he wished. He had his own sweet way with the editors. The days were grayed with his own thoughts.

Yet he was not unhappy. And that was odd, he thought. He was an old man; that is, in this weird business. The newspaper world was essentially a young man's world, and had no mercy on the aged. No man went on forever gathering and writing news, no matter how good he might be. If the war had not taken all the young men away, he realized, he would probably have been given some old man's job. He might even be made an editor, Lord forbid. He would not have an opportunity to return to the battle fronts as a war correspondent. Nobody would believe he was still strong enough to compete with the fresh, young collegians the papers had sent abroad. And someday, after the war, he would inevitably be fired to give some cub a chance.

Too old for his job, though he was little more than fifty-one; and too old, by all the prophets and pundits of stage, screen, radio, and the written word, for any serious thoughts of romance or matrimony! A man of fifty or over should retire, should be past falling in love, should step altogether out of the world of youth. He was a has-been and should reconcile himself to an old man's lot.

Yet, foolish or not, he felt himself still as able as any youngster; and he sighed as ardently as any adolescent — for a woman as lovely and as distant and as unattainable as the evening star! No, he was not unhappy.

And some days were tinted with deep purple.

There was the day he walked on the bottom of a lake in northern Indiana, getting material for a feature story on the work of the Field Museum. The scientists whom he accompanied were equipped with diving helmets, which permitted them to walk under water. They were studying the plant life on the bottom, preparing to make an exhibit. Mr. Dee put on a helmet and went down for a little stroll.

With twelve feet of water above him, waving vines about him, and gay fish swimming all around, he suddenly was convinced that Catherine was ill. He took off the helmet and shot up — to find he was wanted on the telephone in the near-by hotel.

"Long distance calling," one of the scientists said. "New York. Shall I row you ashore?"

Mr. Dee grabbed a bathrobe out of the boat, swam ashore with it — getting it sopping wet — and hurried to the phone.

"It's Catherine," a voice said. "I was worried about you. A friend came in and gave me some money. She said I could do whatever I liked with it. So I called you. Are you all right?"

"How did you track me down?"

"Through your city editor, of course. Do you love me?"

"More than all the fishes in the lake."

"What's this about fish? Have you been drinking, Mr. Dee?"

One telephone call was good for weeks of drab, gray days.

And there was the day Mr. Dee returned to his mother's home after an elephant hunt.

"Bishop Sheil has called you several times," his mother said. "Catherine is in town. And her son, George. The bishop is giving them a dinner, and he wants you too."

"Call a taxi, will you, Hon?" Mr. Dee said, "while I change clothes and shave."

A tall young man in the uniform of a Canadian officer greeted Mr. Dee outside the door of Catherine's hotel room.

"How's the elephant hunter?" he said. "Mother's nearly insane, wondering if you'd get here in time. You got the elephant, I hear."

"Hi, George," Mr. Dee said, shaking the boy's hand hard. "Yep. Me, and a lot of farmers and circus roustabouts and a few score cops. We rounded the elephant up and sent her back where she belongs. So Catherine was worried? Swell."

"Good show!" George said.

George had come all the way from Belgium, but his mother didn't know that then. He had gone there by submarine, in civvies; and had worked with a number of others, installing radios in Brussels for the underground patriots. He had not dared go near his grandmother's home. She might recognize him, might call out his name. And any recognition might betray him to the Nazis, endanger the success of his undertaking — and get him hanged as a spy. All Catherine knew was that her son was home on leave, safe and well. All Mr. Dee knew was that he had an almost paternal pride in the boy.

And there was the day Catherine stopped in front of a store on Michigan Avenue, and pointed to a ring with an amethyst stone.

"At least we could be engaged," she said. "It would make us feel a little less hopeless. If that ring doesn't cost too much . . ."

Mr. Dee kissed it and put it on her finger the next day. They were kneeling before the Virgin's altar in Old St. Mary's Church. It was the Fourth of July.

It was quiet in the church. Candles flickered before the picture of the Madonna and her Child. There was a faint smell of incense. There was an atmosphere of peace and hope and abundant love . . . and resignation.

Bands were playing not far away. Men and boys were parading on Michigan Avenue. Flags drooped in the sullen heat. Airplanes were roaring over the Loop. Thin lines of sweating spectators watched the parade go by.

"You once said the voice of the Bishop was the voice of God to you," Mr. Dee remarked, after they had left the church. "Suppose the Bishop were to say . . ."

Catherine smiled, bleakly. "I've already asked him about that. I've also asked my spiritual director, Father Paul Furfey. Both said I must not marry. The Bishop was the more emphatic. He said I must not marry under any circumstances."

The parade had passed. They walked leisurely through Grant Park.

"Little boys going to war," Catherine said. "Little girls going to hell. God pity them all."

They wandered aimlessly through the quiet, sultry Loop.

"A strange city," she remarked. "With foreign-sounding names. Michigan. Wabash. Wabansia. Huron. Erie. Milwaukee. Winnebago. The Indians have left footprints here indeed. Chicago! I love the city, Mr. Dee — except when you are far away from it, on some assignment for the *Sun*. There are much better papers in New York. Why don't you come back?"

Friendship House, now at 4223 Indiana Avenue, was opened at 305 and 309 East 43rd Street, that year, on November 3, the feast of Mr. Dee's friend, Blessed Martin de Porres. Catherine came for the event, but Mr. Dee saw little of her. The Bishop took up most of her time.

There had been letters, of course. Catherine wrote every day. Mr. Dee wrote once in a while. He read her letters avidly, reread them, tore them into shreds, and let the winds blow them where they would.

But suddenly the letters ceased.

Mr. Dee telephoned New York.

"The baroness?" a girl's voice said. "She isn't here. I don't know where she is. I was going to write and ask you."

Friendship House, Toronto

Friendship House Library,
Harlem — Exterior

Friendship House Library
Interior — Catherine Working
at Her Desk

He hurried to the House on 43rd Street.

"She isn't here," he was told. "Nobody knows where she is, if you don't. New York is worried."

She had disappeared.

Mr. Dee thought Bishop Sheil could tell him what had happened; if he would. But the Bishop was out of town.

On a particularly gray winter afternoon early in 1943, the city editor of the *Sun* stopped at Mr. Dee's desk and interrupted his reading.

"We haven't had a good local yarn in weeks," he said. "The paper stinks of war. Suppose you visit some of those dumps in South State Street and dig us up a feature yarn of some kind. We won't use it until Monday. I was down there the other night. Quaint. Lots of color."

This was "old stuff" to Chicago, though new to the editor — who had never seen Chicago until he was 36.

Mr. Dee put away his book and reached for his overcoat and hat. His phone rang.

It was Hollywood calling. Could he come out and write a movie based on a news story he had written? And how much money did he want?

"I'm not interested," Mr. Dee said.

He hung up with a grin. He hated Hollywood and all its works and pomps, but it was good to know he was wanted there.

He went to South State Street, that little stretch of squalid buildings between Van Buren and Polk. On the wrong side of the street. Dives. Taverns. Gin mills. Catchpenny arcades. Restaurants. Cheap burlesque houses, their front entrances plastered with the pictures of half-naked girls.

The street was alive with drunks, curious boys in uniform, "bums," moochers, idlers of all kinds,

The neighborhood had changed but little with the years, Mr. Dee thought. He went into a tavern and sat in a booth. A girl left the bar and sat beside him, smiling.

"Buy me a drink, Honey?"

A bee girl. They were in most every joint on the street. Their business was to coax a man to buy. They got a percentage on every drink. They were served colored water — which cost the same as the whiskey it was supposed to be. Sometimes the bartender put a drop of Scotch or rye into the water, so a sucker could smell it and be convinced. The bee girls made money for the house, and for themselves.

This girl, Mr. Dee thought, might steer him toward some sort of yarn if he could make her talk.

"Anything you like," he said.

"Katie," the bee girl cried. "A little service please."

A plangent voice answered from the rear. "Service coming up."

"I guess I need a drink," Mr. Dee thought. "I'm hearing voices."

Katie, the waitress, stood at the table.

Mr. Dee looked up and saw the girl he thought he would never see again.

"What in the name of God are you doing here?" he demanded. His tone was savage.

"You don't have to swear," the bee girl rebuked him. "Katie's a friend of mine. She works here. And nobody can swear at her when I'm around. What sort of a heel are you, you heel?"

"It's all right, Cynthia," Catherine said. "This is an old friend of mine."

"Well," Cynthia said, "that's all right then. I didn't mean to call you a heel. But you still can't swear at Katie. Nobody can swear at Katie."

She had sense enough to leave the booth, after a little time.

"It's good to see you, Mr. Dee," Catherine said.

"And it's wonderful to see you. Have you left Friendship House? What's happened to you? Have you been here all the time? You look as though you'd been in hell."

"I'm still in hell," she said.

"Sit down, Catherine."

"I can't, Mr. Dee. It's against the rules. May I have your order, please?"

He watched her carrying heavy trays from the bar to various booths, pocketing a tip now and then, now and then deftly avoiding an amorous paw.

"I'm on a story," Mr. Dee explained when she came back to his booth. "Get your hat and coat and come along."

"Come back around midnight," she said. "Then we can talk."

⋙ 21 ⋘

MR. DEE managed to find a story. He walked back to his office. He wrote it and turned it in. He walked through the Loop for hours, a thousand questions in his mind, a great peace in his breast. Something terrible must have happened. But it didn't matter now. Nothing mattered. He had found her.

He wandered back to the tavern long before midnight, and stood at the end of the bar, watching Catherine at work. She had only a few moments to rest, only a few words to say at a time. She was perpetual motion.

"I'm Katie the Polack again," she said, in one of her frequent visits to the bar. "Two calverts, Joe. A bottle of beer. One gin fizz. And one Jamaica rum and coke. For lands' sake, Mr. Dee, don't call me Baroness here. Don't mention Friendship House."

"Look at that little sailor," she said. "Today he drinks and dices; tomorrow he drowns. Say a little prayer for him, Mr. Dee.

"Did you see the girl in the red sweater? The one with the marine? I'll swear she isn't more than fourteen or fifteen. I refused to serve her anything. She went away mad. So many kids going wrong! Four scotch, Joe, one rye. All with ginger ale, God help them. And a rum collins."

It was after midnight when she could afford him any sort of explanation. They sat in an all-night restaurant on Van Buren Street, staring at black coffee they neither wanted nor saw. Just sitting and staring. Catherine seemed too tired to talk.

"Blame holy Mother Church," she said at last.

Mr. Dee turned violently in the one-armed chair.

"The Church? Did the Church send you to that dump, put an apron on you, stick a tray in your hand, and bid you run your legs off for a bunch of sots and tramps?"

"Relax," she said wearily. "The Church wanted to know what goes on among Catholic workingmen and women, and among the girls who flock around the soldiers, sailors, and marines, and among the fighting men — why so many have fallen away from the Faith.

"The Bishops got together and decided to investigate. Bishop Sheil asked if I would tackle the job. I said I would. I still had my card in the Waitresses and Bartenders' Union, so it was easy for me to get a job.

"Now you tell me how come I find you with a bee girl!"

Mr. Dee explained.

"I'll forgive you this time," Catherine said generously. "But, when I saw you there with Cynthia — it was like the end of the world."

"So you didn't leave Friendship House?"

"No. Of course not. I have worked in a factory, a hotel, a restaurant, and various other places, living as the average poor Catholic girl without a home in Chicago must live. I make reports to the Bishop every week. I keep in constant touch with him, and nobody else. Nobody except him and his secretary knew what I was doing — until you walked in on me, with that blonde little bee girl. And nobody else must know — not for a little while yet. I'm writing a book about all this. I call it *Dear Bishop*. If it's ever published it may turn things upside down.

"But how could I know that some nosy newspaperman would learn this hush-hush secret? If you only knew what heaven it is to see you again, Mr. Dee!"

"You can't go on like this," he said. "It'll kill you. You look half dead already."

"Only half dead? I feel deader than that. It's not only the work, and the horrible room where I live. It's the things I've learned. I'm sick at heart. So many, many Catholics have left the Church. So many, many kids. It seems to me there are ninety-nine outside the Fold these days for everyone that has stayed in. Stray sheep. And nobody cares what becomes of them. How necessary the lay apostolate is!"

The lay apostolate. Always the lay apostolate.

"But," she smiled again, "eighteen people have come back to the sacraments since I went to work in the tavern."

"Wonderful!" Mr. Dee said.

Something of the old spark came back to light up her tired face for a moment.

"Bosh! Don't give me any credit. Don't you know that nobody on earth can convert anybody else? It's only the Holy Ghost that does that. We are nothing, Mr. Dee. Of ourselves we can do nothing. But, with the help of the Holy Ghost, we can do miracles."

She gave him a sidelong look, prepared to enjoy his reactions. "There was a cop who made a pass at me the first night in the tavern."

"Who is he?"

"Now, now. Keep your Irish down. I made a date with him."

"You didn't!"

"I did. Outside the confessional in St. Mary's! He hadn't been to confession in seven years."

"I used to wonder about you," Mr. Dee said softly, "about

your going hungry around New York, getting tossed out of one job after another, being tempted, and all that sort of stuff. Do you always bring the tempter to the priest?"

"Never mind that. Tell me. Have I aged much? Am I thinner than I was?"

She looked like a hag, but she never seemed lovelier to Mr. Dee.

"Where do you live?" he asked. "I'll get a cab."

"No. We'll walk. It will rest me to walk."

"After walking your legs off all afternoon and night?"

"Walking with you, Mr. Dee, is restful. I think God sent you to me today — with or without that bee girl. I don't know how I stood this life without you."

She lived in a horrible little room on Wabash Avenue, near Roosevelt Road. She paid $4.50 a week rent, and gave the janitor fifty cents so he wouldn't steal what few things she had.

She made something like $30 a week, counting tips, she said.

"The girls are very good to me," she explained. "Every time I bring drinks to their tables they make the man give me a dime tip. My name is Katie Hook to them. And you know what they call me sometimes? They call me the Duchess of South State Street!"

Mr. Dee's phone was ringing when he went into the office the next day. Hollywood again.

"It is imperative you come out here. How much money do you want?"

Mr. Dee named a figure he thought even Hollywood would consider too much and hung up the receiver. This was Catherine's day off. He told the city desk he didn't feel like working, and took a taxi to the horrible little room on Wabash Avenue.

They went to the Blackstone Hotel for dinner that evening, and played with turkey and champagne.

"Why don't you marry me, Catherine?" he asked.

"Are you going to start that again? How many times have you proposed to me? In how many different ways? How many times must I say 'no'?"

"That house in Combermere," he said. "Do you think your cousin Nick would sell it?"

"Don't talk about such things," she bade him. "Let me enjoy all this. Don't talk about anything but the music, the wine, the food. And let us dance. I am nearly through with my work for the bishops. Next week I will go back to New York. I — may never see you again. Can't we dance just once together — before we say another long good-by?"

"And I may be going to Hollywood," Mr. Dee said. "I don't think I will, but I may be wrong."

After dinner they toured the Loop. She was shy as though her escort were a stranger. And she kept remembering things — like one who has returned to his native city after many years.

"Van Buren. Michigan. Wabash. Once they were foreign-sounding names. Once Chicago was a city of romance and wonder. Now they are just dirty streets. Once I loved your native town, Mr. Dee. Now I hate it."

They rested on a stone bench in Grant Park, watching an illuminated electric clock as it ticked away the minutes.

"Trying to time the timeless," Catherine said, jumping up. "Come on. Let's walk again."

She recalled familiar landmarks.

"This is the store where you bought the ring. This is the corner where we met by accident one spring day. Was it last year or the year before? You were hurrying to my hotel, and

I was hurrying toward your office. This is the restaurant where we once took George. Remember the fat lady who asked if you were George's father? I was so proud of you when you said you were. I almost wept. I'm going to weep now."

She put her arms about his shoulders and sobbed.

"You don't mind? I'll be all right in a minute. I've worked too hard. I've seen too many awful things, heard too much cursing, too many obscenities, too many filthy stories. And I've missed you so, Irishman. I've missed you so dreadfully much!"

"Marry me," he said, "and I'll buy you Combermere."

"No more," she said. "No more, Mr. Dee. A girl gets tired fighting all the time even with her back against a wall. And — and a girl can die of just sheer weariness. Don't ever ask me again."

There was a telegram waiting for Mr. Dee at his home.

Hollywood thought his figure reasonable. Could he take the first plane from Chicago?

He showed the wire to Catherine the next evening.

"Go," she advised him. "Let me be crucified alone. It is easier that way."

"Christ was crucified between two heels," he said. "Why can't you have one heel beside you? Or why can't I stay at the foot of your cross, and reach you a lollipop now and then?"

They were standing at the end of the bar. Three Negro musicians were playing a boogey-woogey tune. Soldiers and sailors were laughing loudly in the row of darkened booths. A bee girl was singing with the music. Another was laughing in drunken hysteria. Two couples were dancing under the dim electric lights.

"Sometimes I almost go crazy listening to this music," Catherine said. "The same for Table Five, Joe. Six beers for the sailors. A scotch and plain water for the corporal, and a glass of milk for the girl. I'll swear she's under age. Go tonight, Mr. Dee. Go now."

She loaded her tray from the bar and hurried away.

"Hey, Katie," a bee girl called. "Service over here."

"Service coming up."

Mr. Dee went home and packed. Maybe he was a fool after all to regard himself as young.

⇒ 22 ⇐

MR. DEE sat with friends in a famous Hollywood rendezvous, and drank and talked — and wished he were back in a
certain honky-tonk in Chicago.

An orchestra played classical music. It played softly. The
waiters moved deferentially about, without noise. They bowed
to the illustrious guests. The drinks were excellent. The lights
were not too dim. Nobody shouted, "Katie — service!" Nobody
answered, "Service coming up."

A moving picture starlet sat across from Mr. Dee. She was
svelte and blue and golden, and much more lovely than any
camera could suggest. She made Mr. Dee remember, poig-
nantly, a haggard and harried barmaid, and hard, square,
useful, merciful hands. He wondered idly how this girl would
react if a Negro baby were placed within her arms. Would
her eyes shine at some worried Negro woman? Would she
nurse some sick and sweating Negro man — and thank God
for the privilege?

She would be a great actress someday, perhaps. But would
she ever be as great as Catherine de Hueck? Could any other
woman be so great?

He talked of God!

He talked of God only because these friends seemed hungry
to hear about Him, because they kept asking questions about
Him.

Hollywood wasn't new to Mr. Dee. He had known it as a

reporter, as a magazine writer, and as a carpenter of moving picture scripts. But, because he had been labeled a "Catholic author," he was new to Hollywood — and agents, players, writers, directors, publicity men, Protestants and Jews and Catholics, and men and women of no religious beliefs, sought him out to talk to him of God.

He had begun to get a good idea of the lay apostolate. A layman could go where priests and nuns could never venture. He could talk religion to people who would not be seen near a rectory or a convent. He could preach even with his mouth shut — since his way of life was much more eloquent than speech. Or should be.

Mr. Dee realized that his friends were listening to him avidly — only because he was an ordinary man talking to ordinary people about extraordinary things.

The fact that he talked with a whiskey glass in his hand did not cheapen the words he said; but, oddly enough, rather enriched them. In this place it gave him more authority than a crozier.

Mr. Dee became self-conscious. What was he after all but a tough, "hard-boiled," world-suspicious, tippling newspaperman? He had never read theology. He had never been able to wade through the precise phases of the profound and pious. But, he discovered, he could answer all the questions asked him. He had learned a lot in Friendship House. The knowledge heartened him. The alcohol gave him courage to continue.

A fallen-away Catholic spoke bitterly of priests. And Mr. Dee felt close, in that moment, to Katie Hook listening to similar talk in the jive-jumping tavern on South State Street.

"I talked to Bishop Sheil about that once," he said. "Would you like to hear what he answered?"

"Yes," said the movie star. "I would."

"But first," said the director, "another round of drinks. The same, everybody?"

The producer saw some friends and beckoned them to join the party.

"This is going to be rich," he said. "Here's a Chicago news-hawk going to preach a sermon, with a wet table for a pulpit, and a glass of booze for a Bible. Sit down, everybody, and listen."

Mr. Dee remembered Catherine at the dinner in London. He raised a fresh glass in salute, sipped it, and described his friend, the prelate, who loved all youth.

"I was disturbed about a certain priest," Mr. Dee began. "He seemed to be a harsh, overbearing scold. He could talk of nothing but the need for money. He would not allow Negroes in his church, pointing out that if he permitted them there the white congregation would leave, and he would be unable to pay the mortgage. He cursed, at times. He was — well, everything I thought a priest should not be."

"I left the Church because of a priest like that," the movie actress said.

"The Bishop listened," Mr. Dee went on, "with smiling eyes and lips. He wasn't angry as I thought he should be. Merely amused at me.

" 'Of course this is an unworthy priest,' he said, when I had finished. 'Any priest who won't take Negroes into his church, or who discriminates against them in any way, is no true follower of Christ. But — isn't he a proof of the divine origin of the Church?' "

Mr. Dee sipped from his glass and watched his audience. They squirmed in uneasiness, not understanding.

"I didn't understand that," Mr. Dee confessed. "And Bishop

Sheil saw I didn't. 'There are many bad priests,' he said. 'It's a pity, but it is true. There are bad bishops too. There have been thousands of them through the years. And there have been popes so corrupt a decent man wouldn't invite them into his home. Doesn't that prove the divine origin of the Church?' "

Mr. Dee saw that his audience was still puzzled. They waited, absorbed.

"I told the Bishop I didn't see the point he was trying to make," Mr. Dee said. "He laughed at me. 'Of course you do,' he said. 'The point is this, that if we on the inside have not been able to wreck the Church in two thousand years, it must be of divine origin. We on the inside have done more to harm the Church than all the enemies outside the walls — including the Communists. And we haven't made a dent in its structure. We haven't dimmed the luster of a single truth. We have not lessened in any way its power to save the world.' "

"Well, I'll be damned!" the producer shouted.

In the stunned silence that had followed Mr. Dee's story, his voice was startling.

"I see it now," he said. "We confuse the priest with the Church. We forget he's only a man, only human. But why the hell don't somebody tell us these things when we're kids? Why do we expect every priest and every nun to be a plaster saint? Waiter — more of the same."

As Mr. Dee walked to the Beverly Hills Hotel — it was less than a mile away — he felt as though Catherine de Hueck were walking with him.

There was a letter waiting for him at the hotel. An air-mail special from New York.

Catherine had returned to Harlem. She was resting, she said — which meant she was writing forty or fifty letters every day, articles for the monthly paper, Friendship House News, and articles for various other Catholic publications. She was also directing the activities of the staff in New York and Chicago, entertaining visitors, consoling wretched women and children, preparing for a lecture trip, and doing a thousand other things.

She had finished the book about her experiences with the "lost sheep" in Chicago. She missed Mr. Dee. Dreadfully.

"You remember Cynthia," she wrote, "the bee girl in whom you were so interested? Of course you do. She's worried about me. She thinks you are going to break my heart if we ever marry. You are so high above my station in life, she says. I am just a poor Polack barmaid and you are a newspaperman. I should marry a truck driver or something on that order if I want to be happy. Do you know how to drive a truck, Mr. Dee — not that I'd marry you anyway — but do you?"

Instead of answering the letter Mr. Dee put in a call for New York.

It was pleasant in Beverly Hills. The sun was bright, but not too hot. There was beauty everywhere, but not, Mr. Dee thought, a beauty Catherine would enjoy. He strolled through the quiet streets, lined with rows of giant palms, and tried to find a home that might appeal to her.

But it was hopeless, he decided. Catherine would hate this perfectly laid-out paradise of the rich. She would find it restricted and reserved. Without charity. Without warmth. Without joy.

She might accept the painful tidiness of the lawns, the prim and proper spacing of the trees, the precise arrangement of shrubs and flowers, the architectural — and costly — simplicity of the better houses, and the ostentatious opulence of the others.

"But it is a city made for grownups," she would cry out in scorn. "Where are the children? I do not see them playing in the streets, nor on the lawns. I do not see them running in and out of the houses. I do not hear them anywhere. God send me swiftly back to Harlem!"

Up Benedict Canyon, a few miles away from the smug bungalows and mansions, there was a three-room shack, with great violets romping over the yard. Mildred had loved that place. It was not beautiful. It was ill-furnished. It was hot by day and cold by night — but the violets brought little children to the place, and she could talk to them, play with them, tell them stories.

That house Catherine would love too, for its violets and its children.

From that house Mildred had walked, alone, up a long, aromatic, winding road, to a mountain top — and to her death. Mr. Dee had revisited the house but once. And, with a friend, he had motored up the path she took.

The car was parked at the top of the trail, and the two men strolled a little way through the sand, the greasewood, the dwarf pines, and the wild mesquite.

"Here's where they found her body," Mr. Dee said.

"No," his friend corrected him. "It was a little further to the left."

But neither was sure. And — it didn't matter.

"I should not have come here," Mr. Dee said. "I made a promise to myself in London that I would return to this place every year, on the anniversary of her death. Like a pilgrim to a shrine. I was a fool."

"Yes," his friend agreed, "you were a fool. Her death didn't make you a miser, hugging sorrow and borrowing sympathy. It made you rich. You don't need pilgrimages or shrines to remember her. I envy you. Now *my* wife — did you know we were getting a divorce? What's death to that?"

There was no loneliness in remembering Mildred, Mr. Dee had learned — only a great peace. He never returned to the shack in the canyon, nor to the desolate mountain where she was found.

He tried to convince himself he was not lonesome at all, since he talked to Catherine every night by phone. Yet he found a great excitement growing in him, and an odd impatience. He was being paid by the week for the writing of the story. The longer it took him to finish, the more money it would give him. But he wanted to complete the work as soon as possible, and hurry away.

Where should he go? Back to the *Chicago Sun?*

The prospect seemed dreary. His son Jack had returned to the east. He was living in the Larchmont house; Mrs. Kusterer was keeping house for him; and he had become a reporter for the *New York Daily News*. Mr. Dee could live at the Sawyer Avenue house in Chicago — but it was crowded already. He might manage to find a room somewhere else, but there was little pleasure in the thought.

Why should he go to New York? It was torture to be close to a woman one couldn't marry — worse torture than to be far away from her.

Why should he leave California? He didn't know. He only knew he must leave it. And quickly.

The story moved slowly despite his efforts. There were conferences about it every day with the producer and the director, or with the writer who was to "do the shooting script." The director suggested gags, bits of comedy. The story had to be torn apart to fit them in.

The producer had ideas. He had to be considered. The story had to be rewritten, at least in part. Mr. Dee himself had ideas that forced him to make changes.

The day the story was submitted and approved Mr. Dee hurried to the airport and flew to New York.

He had made up his mind. It must be all or nothing. He would take Catherine to Chicago as soon as she could get away from Friendship House. He would take her to the home of Bishop Sheil. And, in her presence, he would settle the matter one way or the other.

Catherine was at her desk in the library of Friendship House when Mr. Dee walked in. She tried to get up and greet him, but she could not lift herself from the chair.

"So this is why you didn't phone last night," she said.

"This is why. I've flown across the continent to ask you for the last time. Will you marry me?"

Catherine sighed and turned to gaze at the little statue of Blessed Martin de Porres, and the vigil light burning near its base.

"No, Mr. Dee," she said. "Not until my spiritual director, or the Bishop says I may."

"I have two tickets on the Century to Chicago," Mr. Dee said. "I stopped to pick them up in Grand Central. I wired for them from Los Angeles. We're leaving this afternoon. I've also sent a wire to the Bishop. He's expecting us for dinner to-morrow evening. Get your bonnet and shawl."

He expected her to say, "Impossible; I have work to do."

"For land's sake!" she said. "You take my breath away. I must call George and tell him. He's home again on leave."

George met them in Grand Central before the train departed. Jack met them also.

"Did you notice the way Jack looked at George and the ribbons on his tunic?" Mr. Dee asked.

The train had reached 125th Street; and it was the first time he had spoken since he said good-by to Jack.

"And did you notice the way George looked at Jack?"

"My son would give anything to be in George's shoes. He tried to enlist in every branch of the service. He stood in line for hours outside the recruiting office. One line after another. But that paralyzed leg barred him everywhere. Once I thought it a terrible curse, that infantile paralysis. Now, of course, I realize it was a blessing. It kept him out of war."

"And my son," Catherine said, "would gladly trade places with your boy, if he could. To be a reporter on a New York newspaper! That would be real glory to him. Your brother Bill took him on a wild ride through Chicago a year or so ago, on some murder story. George said he never had so many thrills, even in battle. He thinks police reporters lead more exciting lives than any other class of men."

"And so," said Mr. Dee, "they do."

They had little more to say during the train ride to Chicago. It was as though they scarcely knew each other, were fearful of boring one another by idle chatter.

Only at the LaSalle Street station the next morning was the strange spell broken.

"Blessed Martin," Catherine said, "we have arrived."

At breakfast in the depot she spoke dreamily.

"I am three women, Mr. Dee. I am the baroness, cold, efficient, busy, devoted to Catholic Action. I am Catherine, a woman who loves leisure, pretty things, luxuries such as hot baths, and plants and animals and birds, a lazy baggage, and something of a flirt. And I am the ghost of a little girl daydreaming under a tree on a hill in Finland.

"The baroness and Catherine do not get along well together. The baroness hates Catherine, and Catherine hates and detests the baroness. Between them they killed the little girl. She has been dead a long, long time. But, you know something?

"An Irishman's blue eyes are bringing her back to life!"

"And if the Bishop says O.K.?"

"She will live again, and the baroness and Catherine will go far away and die."

"But if the Bishop frowns?"

Catherine caught Mr. Dee's hand in hers.

"God's holy will be done," she said.

Madonna House — The Cottage in
Combermere in 1947

Catherine and Mr. Dee at
Madonna House

⇒ 23 ⇐

THEY hesitated, unconsciously, outside the Bishop's residence, and nerved themselves for what might come.

Like a couple in the bull pen, Mr. Dee thought, waiting to enter the courtroom and hear the jury's verdict. Not guilty? Or murder in the first degree? Life in a penitentiary? Death? Or freedom absolute?

The voice of the Bishop was the voice of God, Catherine had said. The Bishop was going to decide. God was going to decide.

They were going to marry soon — or they were going to part forever.

Mr. Dee stumbled on the first step and almost fell.

"Don't be nervous," Catherine whispered. "Trust in God. We've waited so long! Surely . . ."

Her voice failed. She went ahead of Mr. Dee, head high, shoulders erect. She had walked like that into battle many times, Mr. Dee considered.

Words from *Genesis* fluttered through his mind:

"And when they heard the voice of the Lord . . . Adam and his wife hid themselves."

The earth would be cursed, he thought, without Catherine. Life would be filled with thorns and thistles. Or would it? Would there not be joy in doing the will of God — no matter how bleak and hard the destiny that will had planned?

The Lord had taken Marie and Mildred from him. If He should now deny him Catherine, could he say "Thy will, not mine, be done"? He didn't know. Perhaps he could. He wasn't sure. He followed Catherine up the steps.

The Bishop received them with evident joy.

"You are just in time," he said. "Dinner will be served in a moment. Catherine, you're looking splendid again. Eddie, you look in the pink. I haven't seen you in ages. You've been out in California, I hear."

"We took the liberty of inviting ourselves to dinner," Mr. Dee tried to explain, after kissing the Bishop's ring, "because we have something important to ask you."

"Nonsense, nonsense," His Excellency exclaimed. "You don't need any reasons to come here, any excuses. You know you both are always welcome. You've taken no liberties. It is a pleasure to have you here. And now, I think, dinner is served."

Mr. Dee felt alarmed. The Bishop knew all right what the important question was. But, evidently, he didn't want to hear it. He had brushed it gently — and even joyously — aside. That was bad. That was very bad.

There were a number of priests in the dining room, standing behind their chairs. The Bishop made the introductions, and said grace. Catherine sat at the Bishop's right, Mr. Dee on his left.

It was a merry dinner. The Bishop and the priests told stories and related odd and amusing experiences. Mr. Dee listened impatiently. The conversation turned, inevitably, to the war, and the production of war materials. And, inevitably again, to Communism.

"So far as I know," the Bishop said, "the baroness was the first person, man or woman, to raise her voice against the Communists, or to warn America of the danger of Red atheism. Most of us in this country are still asleep. When we wake up, it may be too late."

Catherine talked, and Mr. Dee listened to her, as he always did, marveling, dumb. She was a different personality when she spoke of Communism — a creature of fire.

But this time, he wished she'd hurry up. He was eager to hear the verdict. He couldn't wait much longer.

Catherine spoke on and on; and whenever she stopped, the Bishop or one of the priests, prodded her with a question.

The dessert was finished and removed. The coffee was cold. But still the questioning continued.

And then the Bishop began to talk of Friendship House.

"You've got a wonderful director in Ann Harrigan, Catherine," he said. "The Chicago House is doing splendidly. I hear quite wonderful reports. How is the place in Harlem?"

"Busy as ever, Your Excellency."

"And Nancy Grenell . . . I hear she's a capable woman too. She and Ann managed all right in your absence?"

"Yes, Bishop."

"I liked your report, Catherine. About your activities as Katie Hook, I mean. You didn't miss a trick."

"Thank you, Bishop."

"By the way, do you know there are certain women in Chicago who are trying to blacken your character? So-called good Catholic women! They say you are the highest paid Communist agent in America. They say — well, they say a lot of things. They've written a circular letter about you, and sent it to every bishop, archbishop, cardinal, and abbot in the country; and, I suppose, to every head of a monastery or a convent or a Catholic school or university.

"I got a letter from them myself. I'll show it to you sometime. You'll get a lot of laughs out of it."

"Yes," Catherine said, "I know about those women. And I've already seen the letter."

Mr. Dee had seen the letter too; and he had seen the women who wrote it. They used to come to Catherine's lectures in Chicago, to heckle her.

"Isn't it true," one would ask in a loud shrill voice, "that you are a British subject?"

"Yes. I am a Canadian citizen. I suppose that makes me, technically, a British subject."

Among some people in Chicago at that time, it was considered "patriotic" to denounce the British. These people insisted that England had dragged America into the war, that we were fighting for the British Empire, and that the British were worse than the Germans and the Japs put together.

"And, Baroness," another would ask, "isn't it true that your son is an officer in the Canadian army, a soldier of King George?"

"Yes. He is fighting with the Allies."

"Isn't it true," a third would demand, "that the Negroes in the West Indies are much more cruelly treated under British rule than they are here, even in the South? Why don't you go there, where you belong? Why do you come here, to tell Chicago Catholics what to do?"

Mr. Dee had spoken sharply to a group of these women, as they waited to waylay the speaker outside a hall on the south side; and Catherine, overhearing part of his tirade, reproached him.

"They are just misguided, poor souls," she said. "They really believe they are in the right, and I am in the wrong. You shouldn't have lost your temper, Mr. Dee. And you shouldn't have called them hags and witches."

"I never mentioned the word 'witch,'" Mr. Dee pleaded in self-defense.

"It sounded like that to me."

"Maybe it did," said Mr. Dee, with mock contrition. "I'm sorry."

There was a silence at the table. The Bishop looked at his guests, rose, said grace, and turned to Mr. Dee.

"Eddie, you and Catherine come with me."

He led the way to an upstairs veranda.

Mr. Dee discovered, to his great chagrin, that the palms of his hands were moist and cold.

"If it's this tough to hear the voice of God through the mouth of a Bishop," he thought, "what is it going to be like to hear it issuing from God's own mouth, and me about to die?"

The Bishop saw that Catherine had the most comfortable chair on the veranda. He indicated a chair for Mr. Dee, and sat himself down in one that looked uncomfortable and hard.

"Now Eddie," he said with a smile, "what's on your mind?"

"Father," Mr. Dee began. He had meant to say "Bishop." He tried to change the word, tried to excuse it. He was more confused than he realized.

"No, no," said the Bishop, "I love being called Father. Tell me, is there any lovelier name in the English language? We call the pope by that name, The Holy Father. We even apply it to God: 'Our Father, who art in heaven.'"

Mr. Dee began again. "Bishop, a long time ago you told Catherine she must not marry, that Friendship House was her vocation — and the staff couldn't get along without her. Now we've come to see if, maybe, you have changed your mind.

"We have decided it must be all or nothing between us. And — it's up to you to decide."

The Bishop seemed to be meditating on the proper answer. Or so Mr. Dee imagined.

But, when he spoke, the prelate reverted to the conversation at the dinner table.

"Let's see. You spent about six months as Katie Hook, didn't you, Catherine?"

"Yes, Your Excellency."

"You took a beating. I'll not forget that. And Friendship House took a beating while you were gone."

"Why, no, Your Excellency. Things were all right. Ann and Nancy are really good."

"You've trained them well, Catherine. It takes five years, I think you told me once, to make a really efficient staff worker — and it takes fine material to make a director."

"That's right, Your Excellency."

"People said it was only your personality that kept Friendship House going. But you were away from it for half a year, and nothing happened. I guess it must be of the Holy Ghost, and not of you, Catherine. If it were of human origin, it would surely have failed in those six months. If it was born of the Holy Ghost it will never fail . . . until it has accomplished His purpose."

Mr. Dee told himself he was not being deliberately ignored. "The Bishop knows he has to hit me and hit me hard," he thought. "He's just sparing now. Then he'll hit so hard I won't feel it. I'd better stick out my chin and take it now."

"I'm still in love with her, Bishop," he said softly.

The Bishop regarded him solemnly, then smiled at him.

"I'm glad to know that," he said. "And I think the time has come when you should marry her. She needs protection from those witches — wasn't that what you called them?"

"So you heard about that!" Mr. Dee exclaimed. The fact that the voice of God had spoken had not yet quite registered in his mind.

"Yes. I think she needs protection, and you can give it to her. Marry her, and God bless you both!"

❦ 24 ❦

LAST night we watched a red full moon rise slowly above the distant pine-clad hills. It hung for a long time over the gentle Madawaska river. It lighted a line of Chinese lanterns in the water; and passing motorboats set the lanterns bobbing up and down.

This morning the blue still stream had disappeared, and all the neighborhood was missing. There was nothing outside Madonna House but mist. Yet there was beauty at the water's edge.

Shells lay in the wet sand, opened to reveal the wealth of glory God had lavished on them. Seagoing spiders had hoisted lacy sails to reeds, and lashed them securely fore and aft with threads more lustrous than silver, more fine than silk. The pine needles were tipped with perfect globules of moisture; and those exposed to the fog-enshrouded sun glowed like pearls.

This afternoon the sun is bright, the mist forgotten. The Madawaska is an exquisite blue. The far hills are lavender and brown and gray. The birches are but skeletons now, dancing before the rows of solemn and frowning pines. Through the past few weeks their leaves have dropped like golden rain. But the maples and the oaks in their autumn glory are more beautiful than ever the birches were.

We were married by the Bishop at a nuptial Mass in his small private chapel, on the feast of St. John the Baptist, in June, 1943. The bride was dressed in blue and white, in honor of our Lady. The bridal costume cost her $2.79.

Father Peter D. Meegan, the bishop's secretary, decorated the altar with roses. Long stemmed. Blood red. Fragrant. Beautiful enough, almost, for a bride. We learned later that he took them from St. Andrew's Church, next door, when no one was looking. The nuns cried sacrilege when they noticed the flowers were gone. They thought some impious thief had stolen them.

Catherine Dee, or Mrs. Eddie Doherty if you must be formal, is still the director general of Friendship House. But it is no longer necessary for her to be in active charge. Her assistants keep in touch with her by letter. There are three Houses in the United States, and soon there may be more.

Catherine has come to Combermere to organize a "Canadian province," to start a monthly newspaper, with Mr. Dee's assistance, and to rest.

She rests by getting up early, starting a fire in the stove, going to early Mass and Communion, getting breakfast, spading or weeding the garden, feeding the pig, spraying the apple trees, picking wild berries or gathering nuts, cleaning the house, preparing lunch, writing letters, writing articles, editing the proofs on her newest book, getting the tea ready, entertaining guests, cataloguing the library, arranging the files, going a mile for the mail, reading letters and magazines and seed catalogues and pamphlets, putting the dinner on the table, going for a long walk, nursing some near-by farmer's wife or child, or planning ways to make money for the parish church. At 9:30 she blows out the lamps and climbs the stairs to bed.

The house in Combermere is ours. A tired laundry worker, a hash slinger, an upstairs maid, a lecturer, a literary agent, a barmaid, a devotee of Catholic Action, a foe of Communism, and a little girl who used to dream on a hill in Finland, have all learned that sometimes dreams come true.

The moon may not shine tonight. But we may see the Northern Lights dancing in the skies. And the river may be black. But it will wear bright stars on its sad bosom.

The mist may come again tomorrow.

But if it does, the sun will again disperse it with its warmth and splendor.

OTHER BOOKS BY EDDIE DOHERTY

CAPTAIN MAROONER
RAIN GIRLS
BROADWAY MURDERS
DARK MASQUERADE (with Borden Chase)
STRANGE CRIMES AT SEA (with Louis Bennett)

THE SULLIVAN BROTHERS (movie script)

GALL AND HONEY
SPLENDOR OF SORROW
MARTIN
MY HAY AIN'T IN
MATT TALBOT
LAMBS IN WOLFSKINS
TRUE DEVOTION TO MARY
CONQUERING MARCH OF DON BOSCO
NUN WITH A GUN
I COVER GOD
KING OF SINNERS
WISDOM'S FOOL
PSALMS OF A SINNER
DESERT WINDOWS
HERMIT WITHOUT A PERMIT

Major Events
In the Life of
Catherine de Hueck Doherty

* * *

Aug. 15, 1896 - Born in a Pullman car near Nijni-Novgorod (present day Gorki) in Russia, the second of 7 children: Natasha, who died as a young child, three brothers who died in miscarriages, and two young brothers — Serge, who was born in Egypt, and Andrew, who was born when the family returned to Russia.

       1902 - Accompanies family to Alexandria, Egypt where she receives her first formal education. Brother Serge is born.

Jan. 25, 1915 - Marries Baron Boris de Hueck in St. Petersburg.

       1917 - Fled to England during the Russian revolution. Nearly starved.

       1918 - Liberated by White Russian soldiers. Went to Murmansk where she and her husband were warmly received by the British.

       1919 - Went to Scotland, then to England.

       1921 - Arrived in Toronto, Canada. In July, her son, George, is born.

       1930 - Founded Friendship House on Portland Street.

       1933 - Began Newspaper, *The Social Forum.*

       1934 - Founded house in Ottawa.

       1935 - Founded house in Hamilton.

       1936 - Forced to close house in Toronto. Boris finds work in Montreal; goes his separate way. Catherine meets and becomes friends with Dorothy Day of the *Catholic Worker* Movement.

       1937 - Sent to Europe by Archbishop McGuigan (Toronto) to investigate Catholic Action groups in Portugal, Spain and France. Also visits Belgium, Poland and Czechoslovakia.

1938 - Invited by Cardinal Patrick Hayes of New York to open house in Harlem, at 135th and Lennox.

1939 - Lectured on the Chatauqua circuit throughout the U.S.

1940 - Receives a Church annulment of her first marriage. Begins Newspaper, *Friendship House News*. Son, George, in military service.

1941 - Becomes friends with Thomas Merton who is much influenced by her lifestyle.

1942 - Founds Friendship House in Chicago.

June 25, 1943 - Married Eddie Doherty, both of whose former marriages had ended with the death of his wife.

1946 - Rejected by the Friendship House Staff in Chicago.

1947 - Left the U.S. for Canada where, on May 17, 1947, she founded the Madonna House Settlement in Combermere, Ontario. Her son, George, graduates from Queen's University.

January, 1948 - Eddie Doherty suffers first heart attack.

Oct. 30, 1955 - Catherine and Eddie take vow of Chastity.

1956 - Her first husband, Boris, the Baron de Hueck, dies.

Aug. 15, 1969 - Ordination of Eddie Doherty to the priesthood by Archbishop Joseph Raya

1975 - Her second husband, Eddie Doherty, dies.

1981 - University of St. Michael's College, Toronto, awards her an honorary Doctor's Degree in Sacred Letters.

- Became seriously ill in August and remained such off and on until her death in 1985.

Dec. 14, 1985 - Passed to her eternal reward. She leaves behind her, besides her countless writings, some 21 Madonna House communities: 10 in Canada, 6 in the United States, 1 in France, 1 in Barbados, 1 in England, 1 in Africa and 1 in Brazil.

AVAILABLE WRITINGS OF
EDDIE DOHERTY

DESERT WINDOWS   159 pages soft cover
The meditations of Fr. Eddie, the first poustinik (desert dweller)
of Madonna House and father of all Poustinikki who will come. He
is also the co-founder of Madonna House. Through his desert
windows, God instructed him in the wisdom of the desert fathers.

A HERMIT WITHOUT A PERMIT   149 pages soft cover
What shall the conversation of heaven be like? Heavy, ponderous,
a deep spiritual truth in every sentence? Or will it be light?
Certainly suffused with truth and beauty . . . Fr. Eddie's way of
relating to Jesus, Mary and the saints may just be the most natural
of all. The way everybody's doing it now in heaven.

ISBN 0-87193-005-6

WISDOM'S FOOL   242 pages soft cover
Fr. Eddie writes the biography of one of the greatest Marian
saints of all time. Montfort understood that, if he wanted to know
God, he had to go to Him through Mary, His Mother. Our Holy
Father, John Paul II, echoes this same message in his Encyclical,
Mother of the Redeemer.

TRUE DEVOTION TO MARY   135 pages soft cover
The first adaptation by a popular, contemporary writer of St.
Louis de Montfort's *True Devotion to Mary*. It prepares the way
for Total Consecration to Jesus through Mary.

GALL AND HONEY— The Story of a Newspaperman
300 pages
Eddie was born to be a lover and his love had no limits. He
gambled with life, he gambled with love. The FIRST HALF of
his AUTOBIOGRAPHY.

ISBN 0-921440-13-8

CATHERINE DOHERTY

POUSTINIA
Poustinia is the Russian word for desert. Catherine leads us into a deeper dimension of prayer based on the Christian Spirituality of the East. She speaks of the Journey Inward which every soul must arise and take into the Heart of her Beloved. Over 100,000 copies of this moving book have been printed. Truly a Spiritual Classic.

ISBN 0-87793-083-X

FRAGMENTS OF MY LIFE
In this book, Catherine tells the story of her life, not the purely factual, but, rather, the story told through her interior vision of how God has led and molded her through her more than fifty years of apostolic life.

ISBN 0-87793-194-1

SOUL OF MY SOUL
Catherine shares some of her writings over the years on prayer. It is not a book on how to pray, but a book on becoming a prayer.

ISBN 0-87793-298-0

DOUBTS, LONELINESS, AND REJECTION
This is a book which speaks to our human anguish and how to find meaning in the Passion, Death, and Resurrection of Christ.

ISBN 0-8189-0419-4

DEAR SEMINARIAN
Catherine's wisdom for those preparing for the priesthood. It is quickly becoming a light on the path of Bishops, Priests, and Seminarians. Truly a message for the priest in the church of today and tomorrow. Because Catherine's understanding of the priesthood springs from a deep faith in Christ in the priest, it will always be a timeless book.

ISBN 0-921440-05-7

DEAR FATHER

A message of love and encouragement for priests. In the words of one reader: "In one sitting I have read your love letter, Dear Father. You know my first mission as a newly ordained priest was hard. I felt I had really nothing. I was desperate but said, 'Lord, give me what you think I need.' Dear Father was his answer! O how wonderful and marvelous are the works of the Lord!"

ISBN 0-921440-00-6

CATHERINE'S POETRY AND CONVERSATIONS WITH HER BELOVED — A THREE VOLUME SERIES.

JOURNEY INWARD

This first volume is taken from Catherine's poetry. It reflects her interior journey over many years. This book, with its moving images and haunting revelations, captures the simplicity and the mystery of our union with the Lord of love. Both the intense joy and pain of the inner life are opened to us from Catherine's own experience.

ISBN 0-8189-0468-2

LUBOV: THE HEART OF THE BELOVED

Lubov: the Russian word for love. In this second volume, Catherine presents her life, her deepest interior conversations with God. She never wrote these for publication. They were poured forth, in silence, into the heart of the Beloved. Now Catherine shares them with us.

ISBN 0-914544-60-8

MY HEART AND I

Anyone who ever met Catherine knew that she possessed a spiritual personality with many facets. It can be seen that she, like St. Paul, became all things to all men for the sake of the Gospel. What is it that goes on in the soul of a person that brings her to such a state of spiritual greatness? Read and see.

ISBN 0-932506-59-3

THE LITTLE MANDATE

CATHERINE CONSIDERS THESE WORDS TO BE THE HEART OF HER OWN PERSONAL VOCATION. *Journey to the Lonely Christ* and *Love Love Love* are the beginning of a series, which will be explored for years to come.

JOURNEY TO THE LONELY CHRIST   by Fr. Robert Wild
An exploration of the essence of Madonna House as found in Catherine's writings. The first of three volumes.

ISBN 0-8189-0-509-3

LOVE LOVE LOVE   by Fr. Robert Wild
Volume II of the spirit of Madonna House as found in Catherine's writings.

DEARLY BELOVED Vol. 1 Letters to the Children of My Spirit
These letters, available for the first time in print, form the core and perhaps the most important part of Catherine's legacy to the Church and our own civilization. In them we have, from the depths of her maternal heart, the daily, concrete, nitty-gritty application of the Gospel to the whole of life. They are born out of forty years of great suffering, great joy, and passionate love of Her Beloved, and an unquenchable thirst to pass this vision on to the children of her spirit.

ISBN 0-921440-10-3

KATIA   by Emile Brière
A Personal Vision of Catherine de Hueck Doherty. Many people will write a biography of Catherine. I write from my own point of view — that of a friend and confidant.

ISBN 2-89039-159-0

RESTORATION: our newspaper, published 10 times yearly.

Written by the staff of Madonna House, this paper has been in continuous publication since the arrival of Catherine and Fr. Eddie at Madonna House in 1947.

Subscriptions $3.00 yearly. Gift subscriptions available on request. Sample copies also available.

A MORE COMPLETE LISTING OF CURRENTLY AVAILABLE PUBLICATIONS OF ALL THE AUTHORS OF MADONNA HOUSE ON REQUEST FROM :

**MADONNA HOUSE GIFT SHOP
COMBERMERE, ONTARIO
CANADA   K0J 1L0**